A Christian View of the Martial Arts and Yoga

Brenda Skyrme

New Wine Press

New Wine Press
PO Box 17
Chichester
West Sussex PO20 6YB
England

Unless otherwise stated, all Bible quotations are from the NKJV – New King James Version, copyright © 1983 by Thomas Nelson, Inc.

NIV – The Holy Bible, New International Version. Copyright © 1973, 1978, International Bible Society, published by Hodder & Stoughton.

ISBN: 1 874367 43 4

Typeset by CRB Associates, Norwich
Printed in England by Clays Ltd, St Ives plc.

Acknowledgements

I would like to express my thanks to all those who have in any way helped to encourage me in the writing of this book. From those who have assured me how much this subject needed addressing to the friends who helped with some typing before I was brave enough to type myself.

To Barbara for correcting and suggesting various amendments, and to my husband who fed me with cups of tea and coffee when I was locked away at my desk.

Preface

This book commences with the story of Simon*, a young man who became deeply involved with the study and practice of the Martial Arts; and of the subsequent problems that surfaced in his life after becoming a Christian.

I first met Simon when he came to Ellel Grange seeking help. It was during Simons's counselling I first became acquainted with the details of the background and training in the Martial Arts and Yoga.

As Simon's counselling was drawing to a close, he shared with my co-counsellor Ken and myself his desire to warn other people of the inherent dangers of becoming involved in any of the Martial Arts or Yoga.

During the conversation, someone suggested that a book explaining the whole subject was needed, so that people could be better informed on this whole subject concerning the Martial Arts and Yoga of which so few people have a complete understanding.

I think it was Ken who brightly said 'You could write a book Brenda!' Simon was immediately supportive of this idea, but I declined with a laugh. I didn't consider I had the necessary skills or ability for such a project, but somehow the idea took root in my mind, and with our dear Lord's encouragement, and by His leading, at long last the book has come into being.

* Not his real name.

Contents

Chapter 1

Simon's Story

The following story gradually unfolded during a number of counselling sessions with Simon, and it is through this counselling that an understanding of the dangers of demonic bondage and control resulting from participation in the Martial Arts and Yoga became clear.

These dangers are especially real for anyone who is already a Christian at the time of involvement, and they will also affect those who subsequent to their Martial Art and Yoga involvement, become Christians.

Full permission has been given by Simon to write this story. It is his wish that his experiences will stand as a deterrent to anyone considering any form of participation in the Martial Arts and Yoga.

During his struggle for freedom, Simon's agony of body and mind was so powerful that it needed all of his courage to continue with the counselling. It was his determination to become free to worship and grow in the Lord that enabled him to continue until his full freedom was reached. His story is an example of the spiritual bondage that the Martial Arts and Yoga can have over an individual, but it is also a testimony of the freedom that can be received from this bondage through Jesus Christ.

The majority of Martial Arts and Yoga exponents will not be as highly trained as Simon, or as deeply involved, but *even a few lessons* can open up a person to demonic influences.

When Simon first came for counselling he didn't recognise that a major part of his problem was due to demonic influence and infiltration from a time in his life prior to becoming a Christian. The foothold the enemy had gained through Simon's involvement in the Martial Arts and Yoga only became evident as the counselling proceeded.

The first stage of counselling concerned his early life and the damage inflicted upon him mentally and physically at a time when he was too young to protect himself or escape from the torture he received. The second stage of the sessions dealt with a part of his life where his own actions had caused deep problems. It was only after the first two stages had been counselled, that we were able to deal with the part of Simon's life that had been involved with the Martial Arts and Yoga. It is the third stage that is the basis of this story, but to start the story it is necessary to give a short background of Simon's home life as a child to show how and why he became a dedicated student of the Martial Arts and subsequently also of Yoga.

Family and Home Background

Simon was born into a home where neither parent wanted him. He faced rejection from his conception to the time he was born, and rejection by both his parents and his two sisters, from his birth until the time he left home. He was abused mentally, sexually, and physically by his father, whose verbal abuse included continual negative pronouncements that not only caused Simon to withdraw socially but also caused encouragement for his two older sisters to treat him as an object to be laughed at and criticised at the least opportunity. Therefore it became a pattern in Simon's life that he considered himself not to be worthy of any love or kindness; he only knew that he was called a bad boy and was considered to be unacceptable.

Because of the sexual abuse he received, he was also ashamed of his own sexuality and masculinity.

Early School Experiences and an Introduction to the Martial Arts

At school Simon was bullied continuously and he never fought back in any way. He was at that time undersized and skinny making him a natural target for bullying. He was often left beaten, bruised and bleeding, but his own self-worth was so poor that he just took whatever was given him.

One day when Simon was seven years old, a bigger boy who had been bullying him called out as he walked away, 'Why aren't you more like me? I'm big and strong because I learn self-defence.' As Simon stopped and listened, the bigger boy continued, 'We have ever such a good time at my Judo class. Why don't you come along?' Simon turned and looked at the boy. It was true the boy was much bigger and stronger, and he wasn't knocked about and bullied as Simon was.

The boy could see he had caught Simon's interest so he continued. 'We play games as well. We pretend we are Daleks.' (Daleks were a type of robot that appeared on television in early episodes of *Dr Who*.) Simon's imagination was captivated. Was it at all possible that he could learn to defend himself? Was it possible for him to grow big and strong, to fight back when he was bullied, or perhaps to stop the bullying altogether? It sounded as though playing games would be fun as well. His mind was made up; he would have a look at this Judo class.

This humble beginning was the start of a very succesful journey through the Martial Arts which would include an excursion into the ways of meditation and Eastern religions and philosophy that would eventually have a disastrous effect on Simon's future walk with the true almighty God and His Son Jesus Christ.

The Martial Arts Club

From the first visit to the club, Simon felt that at last here was a place where he was accepted as one of the group without being treated differently. He was just a part of the class of youngsters.

Gradually he learned the moves, the holds, the throws. The playing of games gradually lessened and the practice and understanding in the ways of Judo increased. Along-side the learning of the physical aspect of the moves, he was also learning pure aggression. Even though this appeared to be used only in the practice of Judo, this aggression soon became part of Simon's personality. There was also a slow infiltration into the teaching at his classes, of Eastern philosophy and religions, mainly Hinduism, but also Buddhism, Shintoism, and Taoism. By the time Simon was ten or eleven years old he realised that he could dominate his opponents, not only with the skills of Judo, but also by his aggression. His confidence grew, and his self-worth started to build up. The worm had turned. He could now hold his own with the other boys. His physical strength grew and at last he could hold his head up and face any opponent of his own age.

When Simon was sixteen, he had moved up through the belt grades and became a black belt exponent, a very high level of achievement. He was selected to fight bouts for the English Judo team in inter-country matches. There were numerous newspaper accounts of his Martial Arts activities and he also appeared on television for the sports programme *Grandstand*. He became United Kingdom and National champion, and later won a place in the National play-off squad for the Montreal Olympics.

His bedroom at home became a shrine to the gods of the Martial Arts, with cups, medals, badges, and photos displayed all around the room. He lived for his interest in Judo which had become an all-pervasive power in his life. The sensai (instructors) became god-like figures who Simon relied on to train, guide, and teach him all that he needed in his life at this time. He worshipped them and looked up to them as role models for his own life, and he became a puppet in their hands.

The Enemy's Hold Grows

One day when Simon went to the club as usual, his instructors told him they wished to speak with him. They told him that they had recognised his ability and dedication to his chosen discipline of Judo and wanted to encourage him to increase his ability to 'psyche' out his opponents so that he could read their minds, moves, abilities, weaknesses, and strengths. They suggested that Simon should start to practise Yoga and learn how to meditate, as this would add more power to his Judo bouts. If his sensai thought that Yoga would help him, then that was acceptable to Simon. So a new form of study commenced.

The Enemy's Hold Tightens

Simon learned through the study of Yoga how to relax before a fight, and through meditation he also learned how to direct his mind and thoughts towards the fight and his opponent. He received pictures from the Yoga teacher for use to help him meditate. These pictures were all in black and white. But after some time he noticed that the pictures started to be in various colours. As he continued his meditation sessions, the figures in the pictures appeared to be moving, and they gradually took on a life of their own. The times of meditation took on a completely new meaning, and held Simon's interest completely.

At this time Simon was given a mantra (a word or several words that are repeated over and over again whilst in meditation). The meanings of these words are not revealed to the exponent. They all represent a conditioning of the mind to reduce conscious thought and produce a state of self-hypnosis where a demon or demons can enter and so affect the mind. Alongside this mind-control, Simon learned the asanas, the physical positions and exercises practised in Yoga, and also the yogic breathing exercises.

Next the sensai advised extreme fasting, on a hunger strike level, so that Simon could make his body and mind come under his control and so break the natural cycle of feeling hungry. Simon was told by his instructors that after many bouts of fasting he would come to a stage where he would no longer feel any pain. He was also encouraged to beat his own body (self-flagellation), thus completing the control of his mind over his body. The instructors said that Simon had the power within him to do anything he wanted. He was convinced that he had the power to overcome problems and obstacles, to dominate other people, and even to induce fear in anyone who opposed him by psyching them out. He was taught that in conflict, the issue was to 'kill or be killed'; it was himself or his opponent.

Over the years this training resulted in Simon being able to withstand the pain of breaking his collar bone, fingers, and ribs, as well as dislocating his jaw and having several teeth knocked out. He believed he was completely success-ful in fulfilling the Yoga training, and considered it wonderful that his opponents could inflict damage to his body and he didn't feel any pain. On the other hand, Simon was able to injure his opponents, and at times he saw them taken to hospital with a great variety of injuries. He had it drummed into him for years 'kill or be killed – it's you or them,' and so he felt no remorse no matter how serious the injury was to his opponent. It never occurred to him to discover afterwards how the injured had recovered.

Discovering New Styles of the Martial Arts

By now, Simon's training and dedication had so built up his ki* powers (summoning up of a demonic inner power)

* Ki – Japanese; Chi – Chinese

that he was strong enough to become an excellent practitioner of other Martial Arts forms.

At the age of seventeen, Simon extended his knowledge to studying Karate, Jujitsu, Aikido, and Kendo. The Martial Arts had become his whole way of life, but beneath the surface he was still suffering from severe rejection. To overcome these inner feelings of rejection and a deep desire to 'go into his shell' and become introverted, he concentrated on becoming aggressive, violent and angry and dominated others by his behaviour, and he took to heart his father's words, 'it is an unjust world. Do unto others before they can do to you.'

By the the time Simon was twenty he was introduced by his instructor, who himself was a European Gold Champion, to a man from Korea who was the leading exponent of Ju jitsu in England at that time. It was from this Korean instructor that Simon learned the advanced technique of ki. This involved a lengthy training in how to defy the body's natural protection when hurt or unwell, in order to withstand great suffering without feeling pain.

> With a blow or chop to the neck, he would growl.
> With a blow or chop to the stomach, he would inflate his stomach for protection.
> Upon receiving a kick to his groin, he would withdraw his testicles up into his body to protect himself.

In learning this technique one is quite capable of sustaining advanced damage to flesh, bones or internal organs without feeling any resultant effect. This is, of course, extremely dangerous as pain is a warning signal to the body that all is not well. Because of this advanced ki training Ju jitsu is one of the most dangerous, demonic, and murderous of all the Martial Arts. Basically its objective is purely to kill or be killed.

Mastering the technique of ki to an advanced state enabled Simon to compete in bouts of Ju jitsu with great success. His natural ability and knowledge of a variety of

Martial Art disciplines did not go unnoticed by the instructors and the judges at inter-county contests, and so came the time for the National Committee for the Martial Arts to select a team to compete at the Olympics. As Simon had already become both National and United Kingdom champion in Judo, he naturally won a place in the play-off for a National representative. Before Simon could consider representing the United Kingdom at the Olympics a wonderful thing happened to him; almighty God and His Son Jesus Christ called him to become one of His servants.

A Change of Direction

Simon's invitation to play-off in a national trial to represent the United Kingdom in the Olympics in the Judo contests, and his dreams for success at the highest level in the Martial Arts, did not materialise, because of the intervention of a Higher Authority. He was called out of the world of darkness and the demonic realm of the Martial Arts, to become a child of God.

We praise God for Simon and the witness for Christ he has become despite the battle for his freedom. He did not flinch or turn away from the battle for his freedom, and through that battle this book has come into being.

Some of the Subjects Addressed in the Ministry

It was only after Simon's conversion to the Christian faith that his main problems became apparent, and this is in line with the scripture from 1 John 1:5–10 (NIV):

> *'This is the message we have heard from him and declare to you: God is light; in him there is no darkness at all. If we claim to have fellowship with him yet walk in the darkness, we lie and do not live by the truth. But if we walk in the light, as he is in the light, we have fellowship with one another, and the blood of Jesus, his*

son, purifies us from every sin. If we claim to be without sin, we deceive ourselves and the truth is not in us. If we confess our sins he is faithful and just and will forgive us our sins and purify us from all unrighteousness. If we claim we have not sinned, we make him out to be a liar and his word has no place in our lives.'

When the light of Christ comes into our lives it shows up the darkness, and the darkness that troubled Simon's life was such, that his whole life and relationships were soured by demonic reactions. In the main they were un-controllable anger, especially if he felt rejected, an auto-matic response with violence, uncontrollable urges and thoughts, and almost animal responses on certain occa-sions. Although Simon had made a declaration of faith, he felt it impossible to have a free and close relationship with the Lord. There was a great blockage to his desire to know the Lord in the fullness spoken of in the Bible.

The scripture reference from 1 John formed the basis for Simon's release and all praise goes to God for the work and life of Simon since his release from all the dark-ness that had a controlling influence in his life.

Some Details of the Ministry to Simon

The reader will find some general suggestions later in the book for helping the victims of Martial Arts and Yoga to find freedom, but here I believe it would be helpful for experienced counsellors to have some enlightenment of the type of counselling and deliverance Simon recieved.

Before I write this I want to issue a serious warning to anyone considering becoming involved in this type of ministry. *Do not minister on your own, or unless you have had experience in the realm of deliverance ministry.* We counsellors are called to help the victims of demonic invasion in people's lives, and an over-zealous counsellor without the necessary training can leave the victim in a worse state than when he came for help.

17

Before we began, Simon made a confession of his faith. This was not because we doubted his sincerity, but because the forces of darkness had to hear and understand that Simon had indeed given his life to the Lord; that he was intent on being released from all that had had an undesirable effect on his life, and the suffering he was going through because of the demonic infiltration in him through his ungodly involvement into areas belonging to other faith systems.

We started with the damage from his early life, and this called for a confession of forgiveness from Simon for each member of his family who had contributed to his suffering from birth up until now, and anyone else the Lord brought to his remembrance.

Then we asked Simon if he could recall the negative pronouncements he had put on himself. He remembered saying many things, some of his own volition, and some he was instructed to say by his tutors in the Martial Arts. The majority of the words given Simon by his instructors, were ungodly pronouncements on his opponents, and all were intended to aid Simon in his victory in his fighting bouts.

As each detail was confessed, not only Simon, but we also, asked God for His forgiveness and then commanded all demonic invasion that had affected Simon in that particular area to leave. This pattern continued throughout all of the ministry.

I am giving a list of some of the more obvious areas to be addressed in anyone who has had any involvement in the Martial Arts. It must be remembered that all of these items may not apply to each counsellee. Every case is different and every person's ministry is unique, and therefore will vary.

There has to be deliverance from: all religions involved – Hinduism, Buddhism, Taoism, Confucianism, Zen Buddhism, Shintoism, and any particular gods held as idols from any of the above religions; all instructors by name; the dojo (hall where practice was held); bowing at the beginning of a practice or fighting bout (there is a chapter devoted to bowing later); any shrine, flag, model, flower, or words in the dojo (on a scroll maybe), and anything that represents an idol that may have special significance; the spirit of Nippon over all Japanese Martial Arts; destruction, self-destruction, hatred, anger, violence, suicide, death, murder, ki power, personal damage to any part of the body, and the demon controlling physical feeling, pain and fear.

Since Simon's ministry I have learnt some important lessons. Always start the ministry session with ki power. Not only will the following ministry be easier, but the main power will have left. This item may take more than one session, and will have affected mind, body, and spirit. The other area that will have benefited from the release of ki power is one's own body. Having been kicked during ministry, I can vouch for the power behind the counsellee's limbs, and even one finger pointed at me once sent me staggering backwards until I came against a wall on the other side of the room. This is how we counsellors learn, and by such experiences hope to help other counsellors.

My hope is that those reading these pages will receive a greater understanding of all that is involved in becoming a participant in the Martial Arts and Yoga, and that they will also realise that such a practice is entirely incompatible with a living Christian faith. Furthermore, I hope this book will serve as a warning to parents who might consider allowing their children to join in what may appear to be a perfectly harmless pastime, but actually can carry some very harmful consequences. Allied to this hope for enlightenment on the subject of the Martial Arts, I also hope that not only those considering or already involved in Yoga, but anyone responsible for renting out Church Halls for yoga practice, will have gained some idea of the possible infiltration of the enemy into a Christian Church or building. This is a serious matter and should not be dismissed as an extreme reaction. These warnings are based on fact.

Chapter 2

More Counselling Examples

Lisa's Story

Lisa asked for help with her increasing difficulty in controlling her anger, which was causing problems at work. Her history was apparently without any obvious problems. She had been brought up in a Christian home and had a good relationship with both parents. Lisa had made a commitment to the Lord at an early age, and had attended church services and Sunday School regularly, yet here she was with this problem of anger. Yet she couldn't remember any particular difficulty with anger before she left home to train as a policewoman. She was asked to consider if there was any reason she could think of that had caused this anger, and after consideration she couldn't, yet at work her anger would flare up without any obvious reason or warning. This was causing her problems not only with her work but in her relationships.

Lisa's Employment Situation

Lisa was a policewoman having recently completed her training with distinction, and was now working on the beat and putting her training into practice. She was dealing directly with the public, and had no idea when a situation needing police help would arise. Lisa always had another policeman with her so she was not called to deal with a problem on her own.

She was asked if there was any link she could think of to do with her now dealing directly with the public, but after some thought Lisa wasn't able to see any connection. She said that she didn't feel particularly afraid either.

Lisa then shared that a particular incident had arisen that had finally prompted her to seek help: she and her accompanying policeman were called to an incident where Lisa's temper had surfaced. A man and woman were causing a disturbance in the street, arguing and becoming violent. They had both been drinking, and during this incident Lisa was knocked whilst separating the couple. She realised she was losing her patience and getting very angry. Although she managed to control herself it took quite a while for her emotions to settle down. It was then that she realised this couldn't go on. It was totally out of character for her.

Life-Changing Pattern

It was discovered that on leaving home for training college, Lisa had been unable to find a Church she felt she could settle into, and her regular habit of Bible-reading had disappeared with a burden of studying and tiredness. Her prayer-life had also gone, and so habits of a life-time had changed for the worst.

Lisa then shared with us her fear of not coming up to scratch in her training, especially when facing any confrontation. It became clear that in fact she had faced a lot of leg pulling by the male students as they enjoyed teasing the women, and sometimes this teasing got out of hand. As Lisa was smaller than most of the police students, the teasing had arisen especially during the physical exercise programme which was partly on self-defence exercises taken from the Martial Arts. Here at last was a possible root cause to her anger.

It was explained to Lisa that the Martial Arts exercises

had introduced an Eastern philosophy and religion into her, as all the moves had a background in Eastern religious systems. As a Christian, this was causing a conflict between her own faith and the Eastern religious systems on which the Martial Arts are based. As it says in 2 Corinthians 6:14–16, light and dark cannot live together.

Anger can be a by-product of practising the Martial Arts exercises, especially when concentrating on the self-defence moves, for with practice the moves become automatic and when threatened or attacked the automatic response comes into play almost without thinking. In Lisa's case, the conflict between her Christian belief and the ungodliness of the Martial Arts training, had heightened her reactions. This, together with her desire to prove herself to her male colleagues, had caused her feelings of anger to surface when she was knocked in the street incident.

Lisa was advised to find a church she could attend, and to restart her prayer time. She received ministry for her problems and found release and left with a new freedom.

A section on how to minister to those who have been involved with the Martial Arts and Yoga will follow in Chapter 12.

Tom's Story

Tom arrived for counselling in a mood of despair. He had sought help from his Pastor and church helpers, and had even visited secular counsellors seeking an answer for his problems. Unfortunately he still suffered from severe headaches, and from an inability to remember what he had just read from his Bible. The words became meaningless, and he couldn't even remember the book he had read from.

The church had not only prayed for him, but had offered various kinds of advice. Perhaps there was sin in Tom's life that had not been confessed? But Tom had confessed all that he could think of over and over again. Anything he could think of that could be the cause of these dreadful headaches. Perhaps it was lack of forgiveness that was at the root of the problem? But Tom had forgiven everyone he may have held something against. It was then suggested that his headaches could have a medical base. Tom made an appointment to see his doctor. He was prescribed medication for tension and possible depression. Tom's headaches continued. The doctor made an appointment for Tom to visit a specialist. After having numerous tests and x-rays, nothing of any significance could be found. The headaches and confusion continued.

The Last Resort

One day a friend suggested it would be a good idea to visit a Christian counsellor. Tom was feeling low and hopeless. Perhaps it was a psychosomatic problem as his doctor had suggested, but Tom's friend continued to persist that Tom should seek the help of a Christian counsellor. At last and in desperation Tom agreed.

An appointment was eventually made and Tom arrived in low spirits for his meeting with the counsellor.

Various questions were asked and his background thoroughly investigated. He was then asked to think if he had been involved in anything occultic, or any other faith system. He couldn't think of anything, but then he mentioned quite casually to his counsellor that he had practised a certain amount of T'ai chi chuan. His counsellors listened carefully knowing that the soft styles of Martial Arts in particular, could be the cause of headaches. Tom was then asked how he came to be involved. A friend had invited him to a class, he found the movements in T'ai chi interesting, and he enjoyed the peace of mind the exercises brought him. The emptying of all thoughts and anything that might distract him meant time away from daily problems.

His counsellors explained to Tom the backgound of T'ai chi and the religious root, and how by making his mind a blank, he had allowed other forces to enter his unconscious. With him being a Christian, the confusion in some part was because his mind was trying to cope with two belief systems, and ungodly influences had entered his mind. Part of the study of any of the soft styles of the Martial Arts of which T'ai chi is one, is a type of self-hypnosis; a dulling of the natural mind which would have an effect on the memory and awareness of a Christian.

After denouncing his involvement with the Martial Arts he was able to be counselled and released from the ungodly influence that had caused his headaches and confusion.

The problems caused by involvement in the Martial Arts and Yoga are many and varied. They can be mental, physical, or spiritual. The problems are not always from the roots or the causes one might expect, and so one needs an open mind whilst questioning the counsellee. Here are a few cases and comments that might be of interest.

A Vicar's Wife

A Vicar's wife came for help for a problem concerning her inability to make any sense out of her daily Bible readings. All her life she had been a keen Bible student and suddenly and only recently, the words meant nothing to her any more. She was suffering from confusion in every area of her Christian life. As Chairman of the Mothers Union she had to read any prayers she said at the meetings. No longer was she able to speak her own words and thoughts. Every part of her church work had become an effort, and she was almost ashamed to have to tell anyone about her problem. Certainly no-one would have guessed or imagined that she would ever be confused, for she had been working alongside her husband in his church work for many years without any problems such as this. Her husband had agreed to rent out the church hall for a Yoga class, and several of the congregation including this lady, had decided to attend. It was after attending this class that her difficulties commenced. At first she couldn't believe something as apparently harmless as Yoga could have affected her, but after an explanation of the background to Yoga and some ministry, she was freed from the ungodly that had entered her mind and she returned home with great joy.

An Ex-Soldier

John arrived with a problem that took him some time to share. Although he loved his wife dearly, since leaving the army he had attacked her several times while he was asleep. The most recent incident was the worst. He had tried to strangle her, and their marriage was threatened as his wife had said she was frightened to sleep with him any more for fear of what he might do.

He had been in a special section of the Army, and it was discovered that this particular unit had been taught advanced Martial Arts methods in depth. The men had been used in some difficult situations and as a special force they could be called on at any time for particular situations. This man dreamed of some of the situations in which he had been involved. These dreams had been so real that they had culminated in the attacks on his wife. I'm very glad to say that after the necessary ministry and a recommittal of himself to the Lord, he was released from the demonic hold on him, and returned to his wife a freed man. This took several meetings as this ministry cannot be hurried. His background and nominal faith had to be addressed, as well as dealing with the problem he came for.

Breathing and Nasal Difficulties

Many people who have practised Yoga have a variety of nasal and chest conditions. With yogic breathing one is breathing in ungodly matter, not the breath of God, and the sinuses and throat can be affected. Sometimes there are asthmatic conditions. With all of these conditions, after prayers and confession are completed, deep breaths are initiated right into waist level to completely fill the lungs, and then a hard quick expelling of the breath with an open mouth, will help to release anything of an ungodly nature. Breathe in the breath of God, and expel all that is not of God. A few of these deep breaths should release the ungodly, possibly with some coughing. No more than three deep breaths at a time are advised, or the person will become over-oxygenised and feel giddy. A little rest between the breaths is advised.

These are a few of the conditions caused by practising Yoga and the Martial Arts. There are other conditions, but each person is an individual and will therefore be affected differently, and in a particular way.

Chapter 3

Why Some People Join Martial Arts and Yoga Classes

So many people today are looking for an identity; lonely people needing a personal relationship. Quite often these two things are to be found in joining an organisation or group representing an interest or field of study acceptable to the individual. The local papers have pages of details of people looking for contacts, and chat lines on the telephone are a favourite means of communication for some people. All these things bring people into contact with one another. For those attending a church there are many opportunities of relating to others through the various group meetings, although even in this situation it is possible to attend a Fellowship where no-one speaks to the newcomer; maybe a quick 'good morning' or 'how are you?' without waiting for a reply or further conversation. There are some churches that have in fact become almost a social club with the various activities seemingly unconnected to any Christian belief.

Some people find satisfaction in a sports club or a gym with body-building being a particular interest. Then there are those who join a Martial Arts class thinking that they are organisations purely for physical exercise where one can learn self-protection. Judo classes are of special interest to quite young children, as their parents think this training will be good for the children physically, teaching them how to control their tempers and emotions. Any local paper will at times have photos of proud youngsters having received a belt degree award, or having won a competition. These reports fire the enthusiasm and interest of other children, and as we have already written in the example of Simon, the thought of becoming strong enough to stand up to one's fellow agressor is enticing.

Unfortunately few people understand the full basis and background of the Martial Arts and Yoga. Naturally children and teenagers want to be accepted and to be a part of a peer group, but without good guidance and a loving safety net to catch them when they make incursions into enemy territory, they will become trapped into activities which could possibly harm them both spiritually and physically.

Much of the knowledge and understanding of the Martial Arts is obtained from such sources as the 'Bruce Lee' Martial Art based films, where Karate and other Martial Art techniques are demonstrated, and these play a major part of the story line. The hero always wins by his dexterity and able performance. Many comics and popular magazines for young people depict Martial Art techniques winning over the threatening situation from the 'bad guys'. All the time these books are using Martial Art stances in the pictures, physical prowess overcoming all other odds, and then youngsters take up these positions when facing up to opposition from others, not understanding anything of the background to these positions or even how to follow them up. Here lies a danger for someone with more knowledge attacking these youngsters.

The multi-media of today is continually feeding into people's conscious and unconscious minds that the need to be accepted and make an impression on others is all-important. This outlook is highlighted by advertising, with story lines for new cars depicting 'getting the beautiful girl': and generally making a good impression. Drinking the correct drink with the 'in crowd', adverts for clothes, make-up and washing powder for the 'best' wash.

Women's magazines supply any number of fantasy fictional stories of perfect love and perfect marriages offering to lift one out of the day-to-day routine, and into an unreal world, with unreal situations. Then there are the numerous diets and exercises all suggesting that if you are the right size, the right shape, life will be better.

Is it any wonder so many people have a low self-image, with so much emphasis on what one needs to be acceptable? This leads many people to look for an avenue where they can feel accepted. And so many join clubs and organisations to try to reach a level of achievement which they believe will help them to feel accepted, and be accepted.

There are those who having joined a Martial Art class and following all the teaching to a fairly high degree or level, discover that they have reached a stage where they can no longer be completely in control of themselves. Only recently there has been an incident of a sportsman of great ability who landed a flying Karate kick on a spectator who had verbally attacked him, and all this on a television programme for the world to see. This was a demonstration of the automatic nervous system reacting almost without thought from the sportsman. Fortunately the following legal case came down heavily against the sportsman and he has been penalised by both the courts and the particular sports council with very heavy fines.

There is an insidious infiltration in many areas of our lives of Eastern philosophy, the Martial Arts, Yoga, and various other unchristian subjects. Only recently there has been an introduction into children's lives of 'Ninja Turtles'. A lot of children's programmes, toys, stories, and cartoons have included these Ninja in various ways and guises. Even in boxes of a well-known type of tea there were picture cards with pictures and details of Ninja families. Most of them were frightening and totally demonic. The majority of people, including the head of a children's TV programme, did not know what the Ninja were, and only after having given permission for cartoons

31

etc. to be shown did they find out. There are many fantasy books, magazines, films, Virtual Reality programmes and comics carrying central themes of Martial Art exponents. The words 'Yin and Yang' are used in everyday language, in association with the weather, emotional feelings, attitudes, and even food. All these things have become accepted into common every-day language and conversation.

Yoga meditation is fast becoming a part of society. If someone has a problem with tension or anxiety, they are recommended to attend a Yoga class to learn how to relax. One church in London has regular lunch-time sessions of meditation TM-style* for tired executives and office workers. Some medical practitioners suggest to their patients who have problems from high blood pressure, anxiety, and various stress disorders, to join a Yoga class. I myself, whilst on a visit to a specialist at a local hospital, was recommended to meditate and so learn how to rise above the daily problems in life towards a place of peace and harmony. It so happened that no amount of Yoga meditation would have solved my problem as medical intervention and an operation was required. The specialist was a Buddhist and truly considered his advice to be helpful. There are other doctors and specialists who have advised their patients to become involved in Yoga not knowing the root of that practice.

We can now see how Eastern beliefs and ways of life have infiltrated our society. This work of the enemy is growing, not only through a direct link with Eastern philosophy but also through other avenues, particularly New Age teaching which has certain Eastern roots. It is only by teaching and highlighting this problem that Christian people will understand and watch out for wrong teaching. We have become a nation of passive participants, and passive onlookers of a demonically-based infiltration of Eastern religions and ways of living into what

* Transcendental Meditation

was once known as a Christian country. The m...
Christian Fellowships, and particularly the more fo...
churches, are either not taking a lead, or an interest in
teaching their flocks the dangers abounding in society
from many Eastern-based activities and beliefs. This is
allowing an inroad into churches by the enemy. Yoga
classes are held on Christian property. Only recently I
visited a church advertising Yoga classes being held on
the premises. After the service I had a talk with the assis-
tant Minister and asked if he knew anything regarding
Yoga practice. He replied that they only lent out the hall;
they weren't involved in the practice of Yoga. I pointed
out that by lending out the hall, they were in fact passing
an opinion that Yoga was alright for their members to be
involved in. He said he didn't know that, and was sure I
was overreacting. I asked him if instead of questioning my
words he would be prepared to read up on the subject, and
he said he would. It is only by stepping out in love and
talking to others, that they can be helped to an understanding of the subject.

There have recently been many interfaith services held
in churches and cathedrals. These also lead to a weakening of our belief in one God Almighty. By all means, let us
accept one another with love, but to share our services
with those of a different belief is not a biblical teaching at
all. In Exodus the words are quite clear regarding the
acceptance of other gods.

> *'You shall have no other gods before me. You shall not
> bow down to them nor serve them. For I, the Lord your
> God am a jealous God, visiting the iniquity of the
> Fathers on the children to the third and fourth genera-
> tions of those who hate me, but showing mercy to
> thousands, to those who love me and keep my
> commandments.'*   (Exodus 20:3, 5, 6)

In Romans 12:2, Paul speaks of our minds being trans-
formed so as to know the difference between the good and

...od. In the transformation of the
...titude to a godly state of mind the
...er have an interest in being involved
.... With his mind and attitudes changed
...o God and led by God, knowing right
... many people are lacking godly disciplin-
... ...rches today, and with a lack of spiritually-
l... ..., leading to a passive spirit and attitude, there
is a ... ...r of the people becoming involved in ungodly
pursuits. How many teachers are there that warn the flock
of becoming involved in ungodly based pursuits in the
world? The very task of overseers is to protect the flock
from becoming involved in such things as the Martial
Arts and Yoga, and certainly not giving an example by
letting out church premises for the practice of these
things. For an example of godly shepherding, I couldn't
recommend a better book than *A Shepherd Looks At The
Twenty-third Psalm* by Phillip Kellar and published by
Marshall Pickering.

The lack of concern over many issues in the Church at
large today indicates a passive spirit of enormous propor-
tions. Those of us in the West have a 'comfortable faith'.
We have not as yet been called to face extradition for our
faith, neither have we been sent to prison for our faith, or
experienced direct persecution in any way. This has
affected the Spirit and Power in the local Church, and
Jesse Penn-Lewis in her book *War On The Saints* writes of
a passive spirit that I wholly endorse. In my travels it
saddens me that there seems to be a lack of energy in most
fellowships, but by this remark I do not wish there to be a
false energy or emotionalism either, but a holy fervency
among Christians.

In *War On The Saints*, Jesse Penn-Lewis explains the
passive spirit by saying that the word 'passivity' simply
describes the opposite condition to activity; and in the
experience of the believer it means (1) the loss of self-
control, (2) loss of free will, ... the chief condition therefore, for the working of evil spirits in a human being,

apart from sin, is passivity, in exact opposition to the condition which God requires from His children for His working in them ... God requires co-operation with His spirit, and the full use of every faculty of the whole man. In brief, the powers of darkness aim at obtaining a passive slave, or captive to their will; whilst God desires a regenerated man, intelligently and actively willing and choosing, and doing His will in liberation of spirit, soul, and body from slavery. The text that such believers misinterpret is Philippians 2:13 *'It is God which works in you, both to will, and to work, on behalf of His good pleasure.'* The passive person reads this ... 'God worketh in me the willing and doing,' i.e. 'willeth instead of me' (page 74).

Though this book was written many, many years ago the truths are still the same. The gift of free will given by our wonderful God and His Son Jesus Christ who died for our sakes is not to be taken lightly. It is a miracle of love. Let us use this freedom to be obedient to His teachings and His warnings, that we may be covered by the truth and led into all truth with the help of the Holy Spirit for our own sakes and the sakes of our Brothers and Sisters in Jesus Christ.

Chapter 3

A Brief History of the Martial Arts

The meaning of the term 'Martial Arts' is derived from Mars, the Roman god of war, and is in fact 'The Arts of War'. The Martial Arts as practised today are on the whole, but not in every case completely, a stylised form of the original fighting methods.

From earliest times, there have been various records of unarmed combat. Cave paintings have been discovered in several countries depicting men wrestling with one another. In the Tomb of the Wrestlers in the T'ungkow region of North Korea, there are two wall paintings of wrestlers dating back to the sixth century BC. Many other such paintings are considered to be from the era of 3,500 BC.

Wrestling appears to be one of the earliest recorded methods of unarmed combat and is mentioned in the Bible in Genesis 32:24, *'Then Jacob was left alone and a man wrestled with him until the breaking of day.'* Chinese historical documents describe a form of wrestling from the Chou dynasty (1030–221 BC). In Japan, wrestling is considered to be over 2,000 years old, dating back to a time when Sumo wrestling and other ritual competitions were considered as kinds of godly entertainment, and the outcome of wrestling matches was believed to be 'by divine will'. Even today, Shinto religious rites still play a part in all Sumo wrestling matches.

The Greeks also developed a system of unarmed fighting which was incorporated into the Olympic Games of 648 BC. From the evidence of these examples, it would seem probable that most, if not all of the ancient civilizations, had a method of unarmed combat which must have grown out of the need to defend themselves against an aggressive foe, whether human or animal.

It has been interesting to note through the research for this book that the beginnings of all Martial Arts, as we know them, were developing in two countries at the same time. There is fairly wide-spread agreement that in China prior to the sixth century AD Kung Fu was growing in influence. Meanwhile in India, interest was evolving respecting physical exercises and yogic breathing techniques which later became known as I Chin Ching or Muscle Change Classic. Out of these exercises a Martial Art grew which became known as Shavlin Kung Fu.

In India the monks were quite used to walking long distances, and legend has it that in the sixth century a certain monk named Bodhidharma walked across the Himalayas – an amazing feat of stamina and endurance – and arrived at the Song Shan Shaolin monastry in the mountains of Northern China. Bodhidharma came to China to revitalize the interest and growth of Buddhism, as he had heard that the monks were in a poor physical and spiritual condition. He began teaching the monks a series of yogic breathing exercises which he scheduled into their work and worship routine.

As the monks' health improved, he then incorporated physical exercises into the routine. Kung Fu as it is known today, is still used to promote health, as well as to learn combat technique.

The Song Shan Temple was the first of many temples in China to instruct Bodhidharma's methods of breathing, exercising and boxing. The development of unarmed combat in China grew out of the need for the travelling monks to defend themselves from farmers, brigands, soldiers and villagers who attacked them en route.

In Japan a Martial Art method developed known as Karate-do, or the way of the empty hand. Karate-do spread to China through the Japanese Navy and became known as Shotokan to the Chinese. The link between Japanese methods of the Martial Arts and the Chinese methods came through the island chain between Japan and China called the Ryukyus, and particularly the island of Okinawa.

By the 1930s Karate was a very popular style of Martial Art throughout Japan. In World War II, Karate was taught to the Japanese Imperial Army. When the American forces took over in 1945, General McArthur banned the sport. Nevertheless in the 1950s Karate came to Europe, and now is practised in forty-eight countries world-wide.

Here we see the invasion of an Eastern fighting system based on the religious foundation of a non-Christian belief system that has infiltrated society in both the United Kingdom and America, and indeed into most of the world. This background alone should be sufficient reason for Christians to avoid participation in any of the Martial Arts or Yoga.

The Philippines had their own Martial Arts methods. With the advent of the Japanese invading the Philippines during World War II, many Filipinos enlisted in the US forces. They were not familiar with modern armaments and had such difficulties conforming to army regulation unarmed combat, that the US Army Chiefs allowed the Filipinos to use their own art of Kali and Escrima.

In one incident the Filipinos disarmed a dozen of the top marine combat instructors with great ease. As a result the Filipinos were issued with knives to enable them to fight a particularly vicious campaign against the Japanese.

After the war many Filipinos settled in America bringing with them the practice of both Kali and Escrima, which has since developed and grown in the USA. The art of Kali originally grew out of a need for the Filipinos to defend themselves from continuous invasions. Techniques and training methods changed and developed with this need to defend and survive each new culture that came to the Philippines.

Since the Second World War the Martial Arts have increased in popularity to such an extent that classes for the various arts are now held in almost every town and city in Great Britain and many areas have several classes, each teaching a particular Martial Art.

This growing interest in the Martial Arts was originally fostered by men and women of the fighting forces returning home after the war, with a desire to participate in regular practice of the various Martial Art fighting methods. With this escalating influence in the West the Martial Arts have not only become more competitive but an element of aggression has become evident, which was not part of the original intention. Another aspect introduced to the USA and Great Britain is the much greater influence of Zen Buddhism, whose meditation techniques are incorporated into the study and attitudes in the understanding of many of the Martial Arts.

Chapter 5

Types of Martial Arts –
Soft Styles

The Chinese Martial Arts are intertwined with Chinese religion, mainly Zen Buddhism, and include an interest in Chinese medicine and fighting; Asian ideals which have been formulated by degrees over thousands of years. Short cuts cannot be taken in learning these arts because the training has to follow stage upon stage. As an ancient Chinese proverb states 'He who wishes to know the road through the mountains must ask those who have already trodden it.' The Chinese Martial Arts are not only concerned with learning a sport, but involve a complete way of life.

Because these Chinese Martial Arts are part of a way of life and also a part of a religion they are very difficult for non-Chinese people to learn, although Tai chi chuan is practised by a number of people, and it takes a long study to reach a stage where the movements are exactly correct. For a Christian to participate in this medium is practically impossible. The mind set has to be correct and only students with an interest in Buddhist meditation will find any improvement in the performance of Tai chi. To mix a Buddhist-based art form with a Christian background will cause utter confusion in the mind.

In Ephesians 4:4, Paul speaks quite clearly, concerning there being one true God . . .

> *'There is one body and one Spirit, just as you were called in one hope of your calling; one Lord, one faith, one baptism; one God and Father of all, who is above all, and through all, and in you all.'*

To be involved with Christianity and a different faith system at the same time will cause a weakening of one's Christian faith that will eventually cause problems.

The soft styles are one of two distinct types of Chinese Martial Arts. The soft styles avoid the normal fighting methods of grappling, hitting and kicking. They are based on a system of yielding to an attack and have the Taoist principle of neutralizing any committed attack of the opponent, with a minimum of physical effort on the defender's part.

All the movements are based on animal movements and both the power of Chi and Zen meditation are considered to be of great importance, as it is believed this gives a means of gaining inner strength. There are just three styles that fall into the category of soft styles: Tai chi chuan, Pa-kua, and Hsing-I.

Tai chi chuan

This is the most popular of the three styles and exponents of Tai chi can be seen in most open spaces and parks in China practising the movements. This style is very popular with all ages, and even elderly people are frequently seen practising the slow precise movements and exercises.

In Great Britain the following of Tai chi has grown enormously over the last twenty years. Perhaps this is because this medium is mostly practised on one's own, and this enables one to have a free choice as to where and when the practice takes place. Because Tai chi is believed to bring great peace of mind, Tai chi is taught and practised in certain colleges that teach stage crafts, particularly in drama colleges. The reason for this is because the assimilation of the basic moves is considered to supply a control over the body movements, and calm the mind.

Legend relates how one Chang San-Feng, who was a Taoist and an alchemist, had a dream wherein he dreamt up a system of exercises and fighting manoeuvres which all centred on yielding to an attack. He practised these moves every day and in two years his body became youthful and strong. Chan San-Feng left his mountain home to teach his newly discovered art-form to the people. On meeting bandits on the road he overcame their aggression with his newly discovered skill. He later took on a disciple, Chen Chia Kou, and taught him all that he himself had discovered. Chang San-Feng made Chen promise to keep this new style a secret, which he and his family did for four-hundred years. During this time Chen's family further developed these exercises, and as a result Yang Tai chi was established, which is now practised all over the world.

There are 128 movements in the solo Tai chi exercises. These are, in fact, very difficult to perform correctly although to the uninitiated they may look quite simple. It is necessary to be very flexible to enable one to perform all of the movements, but particularly to turn the upper body whilst keeping a perfect balance below the waist. Substantial exercise is required to achieve freedom of each part of the body so that it can be moved in complete isolation. All the movements in Tai chi are performed in a circle and concentrate on attacking around the circle and back into the aggressor. Any attack is redirected so that the warding off of attacks, and the counter-attacks are of paramount importance.

Because of the difficulty in gaining flexibility in the body, and the necessary complexity of being precise in the moves, it may take many years to attain a high level of proficiency. This style is considered to best reflect the philosophy and the understanding of Yin and Yang. A detailed study on this subject will be found under the section on Eastern religions and Taoism in particular.

Pa-kua

Pa-kua is the art form which links the other two soft-styles, Tai chi and Hsing-I. Pa-kua is based on the eight trigrams which surround the Yin and Yang symbols and represents the subdivisions of creation. These trigrams are also found in the book called *I-Ching* which is accepted as an important book for fortune-telling and is a book of Chinese oracles. This book also contains many moral doctrines and philosophical sayings, and signs of divination. It is said that the trigrams are combined into sixty-four hexagrams that relate to everything in nature.

The movements in Pa-kua correspond to these eight trigrams which create a circle around the Yin and Yang symbols. The emphasis of Pa-kua is upon movements turning in a circle with very few straight line manoeuvres. Students are taught how to 'walk the circle', and in learning this move, they are also trained to gain mastery over Pa-kua's particular pattern of steps. All other moves in Pa-kua are linked into this basic pattern. There are turning and circling moves which involve spiralling and twisting with the body spinning up and down, and twisting from the waist. The circling movements continue until an opening in which to strike is discovered.

In the later stages of development, the internal energy of 'chi' is concentrated upon. Here the 'chi' power allows the practitioner to be completely relaxed and yet form subtle body movements with the help of the inner 'chi' power ready to attack at an opportune moment. The attack is then delivered with an open palm. Pa-kua is both evasive and attacking and centres on blending with the opponent's attack. The training of Pa-kua takes a long time to master, as the trainee has to overcome any obstacle within his own body that would prevent the continuous movement of flowing within the circle.

Hsing-I

This art form is the hardest of the three soft styles and contrasts with the other two by its emphasis on linear movement. The basis of this movement is that the exponent should never retreat, but continue advancing forward. All attacks are made with forceful horizontal attacks with a closed fist punch.

Hsing-I is translated as 'Hsing' meaning form, and 'I' meaning the mind or will. The whole aim of Hsing-I is to link the mind and body together; the short strikes of Hsing-I utilize the 'chi' energy for power and do not rely on muscular development, as mental development is seen to be of much greater importance. Hsing-I reflects the belief that the Yin and Yang work through the five elements of; wood, fire, water, earth and metal, each of which has the power to overcome the other. As fire overcomes water, water can be overcome by earth. Earth can be overcome by wood and wood is overcome by fire. The metal can be seen as part of the basic movements.

There are five basic movements in Hsing-I as there are five basic elements in Yin and Yang. The movements are identified as; splitting, crushing, pounding, drilling, and crossing. These basic movements cover every angle and direction of defence and attack, and there are many variations of each of these moves. After learning each of the moves, the student then progresses to linking moves together to follow a sequence of connected movements.

The last element the student of any of the soft styles will learn is the importance of a number of animals in these soft arts. Each art has its own particular animals involved, and the various moves in the arts will have been based not only on the moves of the particular animal but also on the nature and habits of that animal. Students normally choose which animal's movements and habits they will favour in their studies, and practise these. Some of these animals and birds are as follows; sparrow, stork, tiger, monkey, golden cock, snake, horse and dragon.

There will possibly be other areas connected to nature that may be utilised. A student may only learn one or two of these animal moves specifically chosen to suit his or her ability. The tiger is the main animal move to be taught and is therefore considered to be of the greater importance.

Kung Fu

Kung Fu originated in the Buddhist Shaolin Temple in Central China in the 6th and 7th century AD where meditation techniques were incorporated into a non-violent system of fighting which was evasive rather than confrontational. This system used the mind through meditation, self-awareness, and knowledge of self, rather than a vigorous training programme which opposed force with force.

These fighting techniques became known as Kung Fu and the art spread throughout China and into Japan and other countries. As they spread the moves and techniques developed and changed and today Kung Fu stands between the soft styles and the hard styles, according to which individual discipline is chosen.

The most important features of the Martial Arts soft styles which are opposed to the Christian faith are firstly the Taoist religion which is the foundation for all of these styles, with the basic belief of all that the yin and yang represent, and the main feature of all the movements that are based on birds, animals nature, and the natural habits of all these things.

In Genesis chapter 1 we read that God created the earth and all that is in it, and in verses 24 and 25 it says this:

> *'Then God said "Let the earth bring forth the living creature according to its kind" ... and it was so. And God made the beast of the earth according to its kind, cattle according to its kind and everything that creeps*

> *on the earth according to its kind. And God saw that it was good.'*

In verses 27 and 28 it says:

> *'So God created man in his own image . . . fill the earth and subdue it; have dominion over the the fish of the sea, over the birds of the air, and over every living thing that moves on the earth.'*

Man was created complete with dominion over all other living creatures and as such, to be accountable to God for the caring of all God's creation on earth, to subdue and have dominion. All of the soft styles of the Martial Arts are linked in to the Taoist religion and its teachings, and views of nature and living things that is not acceptable to a Christian view and God's words. The studying of and copying of the habits and nature of any animal, bird or other part of nature is completely contrary to God's teachings and plans for human beings. All men are made in God's image, not the image of other creatures, and apeing and studying the likeness of these animal so as to incorporate the behaviour and moves into the practice of the Martial Arts, will become an invasion that will block any freedom to be all that God has designed for a person, and also a blockage on the complete release of the Holy Spirit in their lives. This invasion is always in danger of surfacing in unwanted attitudes and behaviour that will be at odds with the person's own God-given nature. It will cause nothing but an agony and distress to the sufferer, and a desire to be free from the ungodly intrusion.

Chapter 6

Types of Martial Arts – Hard Styles

The contrast of these hard styles to the soft styles, is mainly in the type of moves. The moves in the soft styles are mainly movements to entrap the opponent by either circling or linear moves without strikes, until coming within reach of the other person, then only using either an open palm or a fist. The hard styles are aggressive, using straight lines in attack, concentrating on the shortest distance to the opponent. All these moves are based on power strikes; kicking, tripping, hitting, and throwing the opponent. The ki power is utilized mainly as a power towards strength that is physical and demonic in its use.

The various Martial Art hard styles are in alphabetical order.

Aikido

Aikido is a Japanese Martial Art that was founded in 1942 by Morihei Uyeshiba. Uyeshiba was a sickly child and originally learned Ju-jitsu to strengthen himself. He was very interested in the Martial Arts and spent considerable time in studying the various systems. His desire was to revive the art of Budo (fighting ways) through good training.

When Uyeshiba's Father died he was very upset and distressed, and subsequently sought the guidance of a Shinto Priest.

One day after a time of meditation, he walked into a small yard, and as he walked he suddenly became aware of a spiritual experience. The ground trembled and a geyser of hot vapour opened in front of him and bathed him in its golden emission. At the same time, Uyeshiba heard voices in his mind and felt as though he was floating up into the air. At that moment he felt that he knew that he and the universe were one.

Later, reflecting on this incident he felt strongly that the Martial Arts were not about brute force without counting the cost of subsequent injury, but were for the promotion of harmony and ki. Uyeshiba set about teaching this new system he had fashioned, called Aikido.

Aikido has a basis of Shintoism, Buddhism, and Confucianism doctrine. Particularly the root of Shintoism has had a profound effect on Aikido, and is allied to Uyeshiba's spiritual experience. The art of ki is central to the practice of Aikido and is considered to be the essence of the art. This power is said to be latent in everyone and is just waiting to be tapped and released, when it will surface as a mental and spiritual power once one has learned special breathing techniques and how to concentrate. This is an unarmed method of fighting, in which defence is of great importance and care is taken not to inflict any serious injury to one's opponent. The basis of the art of Aikido is to go with one's opponent. If the opponent pulls, let him pull; keep in unison with him. If the opponent is aggressive, go with the aggression and turn it against him. In Aikido the fighter does not wait for an attack as in other Martial Arts. The fighter stays calm and serene even in the midst of an attack, and at the same time has the skill and ability to overcome the attacker when the need arises. In this Martial Art it is particularly important to have peace and harmony in the dojo (practice hall) at all times, to help students keep a peaceful control on themselves and all of their movements. To keep this atmosphere of peace, the development of ki power allied to a quiet inner confidence, is brought about through the practice of meditation and yogic breathing techniques. The art of ki is of paramount importance in Aikido, and without this basic element the art would become nothing but a series of holds and locks.

In Genesis 2:7 it says,

> *'And the Lord God formed man of the dust of the ground, and breathed into his nostrils the breath of life: and man became a living being.'*

Therefore to breathe anything into the body which is not God-based, is introducing ungodly things into the body.

Hapkido

Hapkido is an ancient art of self-defence, and was originally developed in Korea by the Buddhist monks who were considered to be the most efficient fighters that were known at that time. When King Chin Hung needed to create a strong fighting force in AD 540 he turned to the monks and requested them to teach a selected group of men the art of Hapkido. The monks had kept this Martial Art secret to the outside world up until this time, but they agreed to train this group of warriors, and they subsequently became an undefeated group of fighters, and gained recognition in their country.

The Martial Art that had started its life inside a monastery eventually spread from the monastery into the rest of the country. A Korean who went to live in Japan to study a style of fighting called Aki-Jutsu, on his return to Korea, taught and incorporated some of the moves from Aki-Jutsu into Hapkido. Hapkido then became a mixture of Korean and Japanese fighting.

The meaning of this art is 'hap-together, ki-power, do-the way'. The main skill is to turn the other person's energy back against him, and this Martial Art is one that is frequently taught as a method of self-defence considered to be especially suitable for women to learn. It must be pointed out however, that the basis of teaching comes from the Buddhist monks, and has the Buddhist faith system at its root, and therefore it will incorporate Buddhist methods of meditation to build up the ki power.

Hapkido spread to America through a Korean master named Bong Soo Han who, in his capacity as an unarmed combat instructor in Vietnam, introduced the art of Hapkido to the US special service group. Bong Soo Han subsequently went to live in America where he set up his own academy of Hapkido.

The art of Hapkido is never to meet an attack with a solid block but to deflect a blow with a circular movement and so take the power from the blow. There are three main moves, circular, attacking and non-resistance. There is a saying that is considered to suggest the basis of this art of fighting:

> 'When water runs down the hillside
> instead of crashing into obstacles
> it always goes around them.'

There is no particular pattern of defence in Hapkido and strength is not of paramount importance, but what is of great importance is that the moves flow from one move into another continuously, until the opponent is completely blocked. This art is very much an attacking defence and incorporates blows to vital areas as well as locking and leverage. The belief is that it is not enough to knock the opponent to the floor, but he must be rendered unable to continue the attack.

Ju-jitsu

In its complete form Ju-jitsu is the art of the Samurai warrior. It means, the art of gaining victory through yielding, or pliancy, or gentle art. Nevertheless it would appear to have grown into a Martial Art more aggressive than the original intention was for it to be. We can see from Simon's story just how dangerous this art can be.

In Simon's experience, some of the dangers arise out of the study of ki power to a very high level. In this study one learns to permit the body to go beyond the natural pain barrier. This pain barrier is a part of the way our bodies have been designed by God and is a natural signal to the body that something is not right. Deliberately going beyond this warning sign makes a person vulnerable to various types of damage, and is the reason why registered instructors have to learn the art of Kuatso. This subject is dealt with later. The danger is for both the participants, and on occasion leads to one of the fighters being taken from the scene on a stretcher to hospital. The aggression built up by this advanced study of ki power can quite often get out of hand.

1 Corinthians 9:24–27 speaks of athletes training their bodies to win a race but Paul says we do it for a heavenly reward. Paul is refering to disciplining our minds and bodies to conform to a Christian way of life, with Christian attitudes and actions. These are all based on love, not on harming other people physically to show ourselves the winner. Our rewards of running the race to win are in heaven.

The art of Ju-jitsu dates back into antiquity, having been known by several names over the years. A man named Akiyama is considered to have been involved in the introduction and development of Ju-jitsu. A tale is told of how he was once was walking in a forest, when suddenly a strong gale blew down a pine tree which was broken into pieces. At the same time, a willow tree standing nearby was bending in the wind and did not break with the force of this strong gale. This incident so impressed Akiyama, that it became the basis of a Martial Art called Yoshin-ryu, or willow tree school.

A basic system of Ju-jitsu was founded in 1532 and became part of the Samurai training.

Although Ju-jitsu is mainly an unarmed combat system, some schools do use a bo staff and yari (spear). The moves consist of kicks, punches, arm locks, and joint manipulations, and in fact this style has no further resemblance to a 'gentle art'. Another branch of Ju-jitsu is Atemi, which is the art of using pressure points on joints, and other vulnerable nerve centres in the body. When these nerve centres are put under the correct pressure, they can incapacitate a person and even cause death. A mixed variety of moves is sometimes used, as all are considered a means of protecting oneself from an unwarranted attack.

Many women learn this art and become very efficient in this style. Ju-jitsu can become a devastating medium of fighting and is possibly the most violent of the Martial Arts practised by the majority of people. Limbs can be easily dislocated and broken through joint manipulation if pressure is maintained beyond the initial pain, and one can quickly lose consciousness with any of the holds against the throat and other means of applying holds on pressure points. This is also a sport that calls for fully trained instructors in the art of Kuatso already written on in Hapkido.

Judo

Judo's origins are in Ju-jitsu dating from the 17th century, and Judo is essentially a competitive style of Martial Art. Karo who devised this art said, 'Judo is the way to the most effective use of both physical and spiritual strength through the training, and you are able to perfect yourself and contribute something of value to the world.' Isn't this the most amazing statement? I personally have yet to understand exactly what the proponents of this art are able to give to the world.

Judo is an unarmed Martial Art from Japan. This method was devised by a Dr Jigora Karo in 1882 and was first demonstrated and practised in Tokyo. Karo looked for a responsibility toward society, and at the same time a development of self-protection through the correct training, in the using of throws, holds, and leverage. Judo is a sporting art, and at the same time a spiritual discipline. Very few people at the commencement of their training realise this last feature, and I'm sure that parents of children joining the Judo classes know nothing of this background. The fact is that whether this matter of spiritual discipline is made known or not, it is the backbone of this Martial Art and the instructors will have a complete knowledge of this fact.

Karo believed that Judo was a good means of developing physical fitness, and it is reliant on the play of emotions and exertion of the will. An old Judo saying says ... 'Fall down seven times, and stand up eight'.

Judo is such a widely popular Martial Art form that it is practised in nearly every country in the world. The majority of people who start learning the Martial Arts, start with Judo, and in 1964 Judo was the first Martial Art form to be introduced into the Olympic competitions. Now it is a regular event. There are mainly three categories in Judo; Tachiwaza (standing technique), Newaza (ground technique), and Atemiwaza (vital point technique). Within these three groups are several sub-divisions.

A judo match is won by one point and this point may be gained by various means: a clean throw, by controlling an opponent on the ground for 30 seconds, or a surrender by an arm lock or strangle hold. If a point is not gained by either participant, the referee can make an award for aggressiveness, which means a good fighting spirit. Although Judo may be considered to be one of the milder forms of Martial Arts and suitable for beginners, at a more advanced level one can frequently suffer quite severe injuries from the various throws such as dislocation of joints from the arm locks, and it is therefore interesting that most children start their Martial Art training in Judo. This alone demonstrates the lack of knowledge and understanding of the content and meaning behind the Martial Arts.

Most of the Judo practice consists of free sparring or randori. Here two contestants practise throwing and grappling according to the rules of a contest. Although practice throws should only be practised in the practice hall, it has been known for children to practise these moves on friends and foes alike, sometimes with disastrous results. Randori will be an all out effort by each student to outdo the opponent. This method is the most useful and valuable of all Judo methods for learning by practise, and building up an aggressive spirit in the students. The students may use any method in the randori as long as they don't harm one another! Karo said that the mental training can be done as well in randori as in kata. Kata is a linking of movements for practise purposes, and it is to build up co-ordination and balance with an ability to flow from one movement into the next.

Although students will very rarely start their Martial Arts studies with Ju-jitsu it must be understood that the inherent dangers of Judo are there even more for Ju-jitsu, as this method is the most dangerous and violent of all the styles, except for Ninja, which takes a separate study later in this book. The ungodly attitudes of both Ju-jitsu and Judo are a source of many undesirable effects in Christians, such as confusion of mind, headaches, and other varied problems.

Karate

Although, as we have already seen, unarmed fighting is believed to have originated in India, the Martial Arts spread to China, then Okinawa and on to Japan. In Okinawa Karate was developed. At that time a complete ban was placed on the carrying of any type of weapon, so the inhabitants of Okinawa readily accepted a method of Martial Art that would provide them with a means of protecting themselves without breaking the law.

Many stories circulated concerning the power, skill and strength of those following the teaching of Karate. Some of the stories concerned the masters of the art and their punching power. One story told of a master so determined to increase the power of his punch, that he went into the forest and punched the same tree every day until he could bury his fist up to his elbow in that tree trunk. These stories fuelled the determination of many followers of this art, and supplied them with the determination to become as strong as these masters.

Most of the developing moves originated from the islanders who were involved in fighting off the Japanese tyrants who had invaded the island. These islanders utilised kicks that could unseat a mounted Japanese warrior, and so hardened were the heels of these fighters, that their kick could penetrate the leather armour of the invading warriors and so strike a vital point on the warrior's body and kill him.

Stories of the Okinawa's powers of fighting reached Japan and they became very interested in the Okinawan method of unarmed fighting. A master of this fighting art was invited to Japan to put on a display for the Emperor himself. So great was the interest in the Emperor's invitation, that an Okinawan master of Karate named Sichin Funakashi set up a demonstration for the Emperor. Following this display Sichin Funakashi opened a school in Japan and called the school Shotokan, or the club of Shoto. 'Kan' means hall, and 'shoto' was the pen name used by Sichin Funakashi when he wrote poetry. This fighting method eventually became known as Karatedo, or way of the empty hand. The Japanese already had the Martial Art of Ju-jitsu, and Korean Tae Kyon, and so they modified Ju-jitsu and restyled Tae Kyon, to become Tae Kwondo and this is the name of the modern form of Korean Karate.

These Oriental forms of fighting were then introduced by USA troops returning home from Japan, Korea, and Okinawa at the end of the Second World War. There are now more than one hundred forms and styles of Karate. In perhaps a hundred different ways all Karate styles are alike, and yet in many ways they differ, perhaps only in the slightest moves. In Japan alone there are 70 styles of Karate which are known as Karate-do (empty handed way). The primary emphasis being on perfecting the character. The 'Do' of Karate, Kendo, Judo, Aikido, Iaido, and Kyudo translate as 'the path', or way and designates that the practise of these disciplines is a way or path to travel throughout life to achieve the ultimate perfection of human character.

The Karate empty handed way is explained in a Zen Buddhism saying which has great significance to its followers:

> 'As a mirror's polished suface reflects whatever stands before it and a quiet valley carries even small sounds, so must the student of Karate render his mind empty of selfishness and wickedness, in an effort to react appropriately towards anything he might encounter. This is the meaning of 'Kara' or empty in Karate.'   (Funa Kashi)

The Chinese concept of 'Mushin no shin' (mind of no mind) means totally immune to outside influence. An immunity extending to reacting instinctively to a sixth sense.

It is claimed that Karate-do when taught correctly is a balanced system of physical education, spiritual discipline, self-defence and competitive sport.

The first level of training is known as 'Gyo'. At this level you will be introduced to the fundamentals of Karate, the techniques, customs, and etiquette, and a complete dedication is expected towards learning the complete art of Karate. The techniques must be practised repeatedly over long periods of time so as to gain the necessary level of ability. The teacher often will seem very critical and demanding but this is the earliest stage, and the student has to learn self-discipline, patience, and perseverance.

The second level of training is called 'Shugyo' (physical and mental mastery and austerity). The word indicates rigorous training in Shinto or Buddhist religious discipline. During this stage the Martial Art training takes on a semi-spiritual nature. By the time you reach this stage, you will have a good foundation of the basic techniques and the focus will be on uninterrupted training.

The third level of training is known as 'Jutsu' or art stage. At this stage the trainee will have the mastery of all the basic skills and will be able to perform almost every technique. Here there will be a polishing of all the previous training and moves.

The fourth level is known as 'Do' level. At this level training will concentrate on rising above outer forms, both physically and spiritually. This is a stage of actualisation, or self-realisation. It is this stage that is equivalent to the Zen Satori (enlightenment):

'Karate begins in the mind; Karate ends in the mind.'
(Author unknown)

When 'Do' level is reached the mind, decisions and actions become one, and the moves are made automatically according to the opponent's challenge. Modern Karate incorporates high kicks and punches, and is a very physical style of art. Those who are fully trained are called 'Karateka'.

Most of the Karate dojos have a Shinto or Buddhist shrine close to the Kamiza 'upper seat' and the students will bow to the shrine at the commencement of the practise session or performance. When one has reached the stage when automatic reflex action comes into play, this can be a problem in every-day life outside the dojo.

If annoyed or frightened by someone, an automatic reaction of challenge can be struck. The mind at this stage is so conditioned by the training that there is no room for any other type of study or actual thought on any other subject. The Karateka will have become absorbed by the complete training involved in Karate.

Kendo

Kendo means the way of the sword, and its roots are based on the fighting system of the Samurai warriors. The Samurai were the cream of the fighters of ancient times, and were held in great regard by the Japanese. These fighting systems became incorporated into the other styles of Martial Arts, and so instead of directing their aggression directly against the enemy, the other disciplines taught their students to utilise an inner strength to unite mind and body and build up their self-discipline.

Kendo is a Martial Art form directly linked with Kenjutsu, whose sole aim was to kill the enemy. The Samurai warrior-class, fought with a long sword called 'katana'. The sword was held in very great regard in those days, and was known as the soul of the warrior. In studying Kendo, the student cannot escape from the original belief in the sword's power, as Kendo is still an armed art. At one time the sword had a sharp blade, but it was decided in AD 400 to replace the sword with a bokuto for greater safety. The bokuto is a piece of heavy red oak with the shape, weight and balance of a real sword. Although the bokuto was safer than a real sword, it could and did, still cause injury. In 1868 an edict was issued banning the wearing of swords in public, and so Kendo changed.

The next replacement for the bokuto was a shinai. The shinai consists of four bamboo strips held together with cord at certain points and at the end with a leather guard to protect the hands. At the same time that the shinai was introduced, protective clothing was selected to protect the fighter from head to foot. Where the majority of Martial Art uniforms are white tunics tied with a belt of the colour denoting the level reached in that particular style, and loose white trousers, the uniform for Kendo consists of a black cotton jacket and an ankle length split skirt. These are very wide and are called a hakama. The armour is called a tare or bogu and is a waist and groin protector. The 'do' is the breastplate made of either fibre or bamboo covered in leather, and lacquered. A wide headband called a Tenugui is wrapped around the head to soak up any perspiration. Next comes a face mask, or 'men', rigidly constructed from steel or nickel with grille-like bars running horizontally across the face. The 'men' has a padded addition to cover the throat. Finally the fighter wears a type of gauntlet to protect the hands.

A ritual is performed whilst putting on the uniform, and this is always done in a kneeling position. Each piece of the uniform is always put on in the same order. The gauntlets are the last item to be donned, and then the shinai is picked up.

During the fighting all of the movements are of a cutting with the blade, the movement being a fierce swipe directed strongly towards the throat. In Kendo competition cuts to the legs are banned.

It takes a long training to reach the first grade in Kendo. This first degree called 'shodan' is black belt, and can take up to five years to attain. The teachers do award some minor grades prior to attaining shodan status and these are called kyu grades. All methods of Kendo are based on Zen Buddhism and are claimed to be ways of self-improvement. In certain places swords of varying lengths are used to fight with, but these are not generally accepted, and where swords are used, the fights will take place outside of a formal practice hall.

The title 'shodan' will bring back memories of certain films which were called by that name, and Karate and Kendo methods have been the centre of several stories shown in films over the years. This again has caused an interest in the whole area of the Martial Arts, especially as Bruce Lee was one of the stars taking the lead in these films, and he was an advanced student of several Martial Art forms. Young people have been influenced by these films, and can be seen practising dangerous kicks and punches without thought for the danger to other people. The more people are informed of the dangers of the moves, especially the uninitiated, and the religous background the more chance there is of an understanding and personal responsibility being taken.

Kuatsu

Kuatsu is a highly specialised form of resuscitation and has many variations. Most teachers have had to take a study course in this subject. Particularly teachers of Jujitsu are expected to study Kuatsu as it is considered to be first-aid of very great importance. Originally it was believed to have numerous methods of secret knowledge, and an exponent had to pass an examination before learning the secrets. Most choking and groin injuries can be dealt with by the art of Kuatsu, but strangulation and other extreme damage has to be dealt with in another way. Kuatsu is not generally known of and only advanced students will know of its existence. The very fact of the need for a specialised method of resuscitation, demonstrates the inherent dangers of the Martial Arts, especially in the areas of strangulation, and groin injuries, but despite this first-aid treatment some of the injured have to go to hospital for a more specialised type of help.

Sumo Wrestling from Japan

Sumo wrestling is one of the styles of the Martial Arts and is included here to not only demonstrate the importance of the Shinto religion to this art, but also because wrestling is one of the oldest styles of fighting man-to-man that is recorded. In Genesis we find the story of Jacob wrestling with a man, and in chapter 32:22–32 we can read the whole story. The result was that Jacob's hip was put out of place.

Different styles of wrestling can be found throughout

the British Isles, and each area has its own particular style, differing in the rules, throws, and holds. In the British Isles wrestling does not have any religious significance, and is not known for causing any notable damage to the participants. It could be said to be a more natural way of confrontation between two people. Children especially wrestle together as an almost natural method of fighting, but in Japan wrestling has very strong religious roots and the preliminary ritual sometimes takes longer than the fighting bout.

The origins of Sumo wrestling reach far back into folk lore and myth and are recorded in the Ko-ji-ki, a very old Japanese literary document. This writing relates how two deities were engaged in an empty-handed method of fighting. Although much of this story is grounded in myth it does show that a method of unarmed combat took place hundreds of years ago, and was used to settle disputes. This method of settling disputes is known of in other countries, but the difference with Japanese Sumo wrestling, is that it has become a National sport, of significant interest, with a style of its own, and a strong Shinto religious background.

There is a story of a man of very great strength whose name was Kuyehaya, who was apparently a giant, and carried out great feats of strength. The Emperor wanted someone to come forward to contest the claims of strength Kuyehaya made, and one man offered his services. His name was Sakune, and subsequently a dual took place between the two men. Such was the strength of these two men that when they kicked one another they both suffered broken bones. Sakune was the eventual winner of the dual by killing the giant. A celebration is still held every 7th July in remembrance of this dual, which is considered to be the first Sumo match.

In 1684 Sumo wrestling was accepted as a Martial Art and a sport, and with the drawing up of rules and regulation, supervisors were elected to oversee as referees of the fighting bouts. It was decided to give the best Sumo fighters Samurai status.

This form of Martial Art is divided into divisions according to the ability of the wrestler and comes under the overall control of the Tokyo Ozumo Kokai. Today the controlling body is called the Japan Suma Association.

The highest award for a Sumo wrestler is the Emperor's Cup. This is in recognition of the wrestlers advanced ability.

The size and weight of fighters is of extreme importance and whilst in training they live in designated centres called 'Sumo Stables'. There they are cared for with a special diet designed to build up the weight below the waist, on the hips, legs, and stomach, so that the weight is set low in the body to help the centre of gravity for stability in fighting. They have to train every day and are set apart from ordinary life so that their whole life is centred on improving their wrestling prowess. All Japanese born men who become Sumo wrestlers and become Sumatori, wear their hair in a top-knot on top of the head. This shows that they have reached a standard of fighting called Maku-uchi which is the top grade in Sumo. The Sumo wrestler never dresses his own hair; this is dressed by a specially trained hairdresser who is in charge of the hair being dressed correctly. If a Sumatori loses more than eight consecutive bouts he is expected to retire, and then on his retirement his top-knot is cut off by his patrons.

The fighters fight almost naked, except for a heavy loin-cloth consisting of 10 yards of heavy silk material that is two feet wide. This material is folded into four, and then is wrapped around rather like a baby's napkin around the groin and waist. This cloth is called a mawashi. The fight takes place in an area called the dohyo which measures four to five metres in diameter. Before the fight can take place there is a ceremonial performance of clearing the whole area of any undesirable spirits. This ceremony consists of the scattering of salt and with much stamping of the feet to frighten the unwanted spirits. The whole ceremony takes at least four minutes to complete. A Shinto priest attends all Sumo bouts and the most important bouts are actually held in a Shinto temple. The object of the fight is to either, throw, push, or pull one's opponent so that he falls outside or inside the arena, and where a part of his body above the knee touches the ground. There are no draws allowed, and if there is a tie, another bout is arranged.

This Martial Art clearly demonstrates the importance of the Shinto religion to this art form, and originally all Sumo bouts were held in a Shinto temple. The exact meaning for this is not clear but one can assume that the gods are invoked for a successful conclusion. The very fact of a priest being in attendance at all matches, speaks for itself of this religious basis. As Sumo is televised in this country, I believe viewers should know of these details.

Taekwon-do

This is a Korean Martial Art and originated in Silla at the Southern tip of the Korean peninsula. Because this kingdom was under constant threat from its two neighbours, it was necessary to build up a fighting force.

The roots of Taekwon-do go back 1,400 years and have developed into the modern methods of fighting. The élite class of warriors at that time undertook to follow a path of training to strengthen Silla's fighting force, and a code was set by a Korean Buddhist monk and scholar named Won Kang. These are his set of codes:

1. Be loyal to your king.
2. Be obedient to your parents.
3. Be honourable to your friends.
4. Never retreat in battle.
5. Make a just kill.

The warriors practised with spear, bow, sword, and hook. These implements and many of the local methods of unarmed fighting, were incorporated into the art of Taek kyon.

In AD 953 the kingdom of Silla was overcome by the Koryo dynasty, and during this time an annual contest was held in unarmed combat. Twenty-four postures had to be mastered by all contestants and these included hand and leg techniques, together with falling, rolling, jumping and pulling.

In recent times (1909–1945) all Martial Arts were forbidden in Korea, but Taek kyon was kept alive secretly. After World War II a Korean named Choi realised Korea's need for a Martial Art and so he incorporated Taek kyon, Soo Bak-gi and Karate with many new techniques refined by himself, and so Taekwon-do was born. The official date of the launch for this new Martial Art was 11th April 1955. It now has governmental recognition as a national sport. This art teaches a defensive method of combat with effective self-defence. The five most important points are courtesy, integrity, perseverance, self-control and an indomitable spirit. The practice hall is called a do jang, and the practice suit a dobak. The jacket is white edged with black, and the trousers white. There are the normal coloured belts for the various levels of proficiency.

Training consists of practising in lines for the basic exercises and techniques, and familiarity with 69 of the vital points on the body which are classified as major and minor. Blows to major points on the body can cause fatalities or permanent damage or deformity, and blows to the minor points can cause severe pain and malfunctioning of the organs.

The most typical Korean section of the syllabus is foot sparring, which is directly developed from Taek kyon where no hand techniques are allowed. These include a side-piercing kick, reverse-turn kick, a hooking kick, as well as mid-air kicks. Advanced students can launch themselves 10 feet into the air and deliver a number of kicks whilst still in mid-air. The patterns of movement are called tul, and the practice of tul allows the use of potentially very dangerous moves to be used in perfect safety, culminating through the various patterns, to using the necessary defensive pattern without conscious thought, so the reaction becomes automatic and instinctive.

To gain a high degree of physical power it is necessary to refine the reaction force, concentration, equilibrium, breath control, and speed. With practice and application Taekwon-do punches and kicks become even faster than normal reflex time. They are therefore impossible to block unless detected beforehand, and so students are trained to always look at the opponent's eyes, and never at their arms and legs. This way they learn to read the opponent's intentions. To test a student's power a test is given, using pieces of wood, or roofing tiles, for the student to break with one blow of the hand. Taekwon-do lays particular stress in its training, on destruction techniques.

One can now see clearly the basis of this Martial Art which is one of, and for, destruction. Unfortunately a number of films, cartoon strips, and comic characters that show this type of Art, show the power of the victor over his adversary, and have introduced many children and young people to kicking and other dangerous moves. Unless parents explain the basis and dangers of this behaviour, it can become dangerous to themselves and others. The fact is that in training for this Martial Art, many injuries occur to the participants, and only the very advanced become truly able to carry out these moves. In the Bible Psalm 35:4, says this:

> *'Let those be put to shame and brought to dishonour*
> *Who seek after my life;*
> *Let those be turned back and brought to confusion*
> *Who plot my hurt.'*

The fact is that even though in practice the intent is to win the bout, there is also a desire to stop the opponent by putting them out of action, and all the learned moves, including the pressure holds that are used, are a violence that I consider dangerous and ungodly.

Ninjutsu

This Martial Art has been left until last for a very good reason. Ninjutsu comes from a way of life, and the art was passed on from one generation to another. It was considered to be an art form where the basic training commenced as soon as a child could stand. It is the most violent and dangerous of all the Martial Arts, and this is by definition and practice. In the hands of the untutored, Ninja becomes death and havoc, and its very potential for severely damaging an opponent makes the training very important.

At this time, all books on Ninja have been banned from the local library as some of its methods have been adopted by those who are out to cause violence and terror in society. Because of this, some of the history will be given without any of the details of the actual moves.

Ninjutsu comes from Japan, where a long time ago a superb group of warriors emerged, whose skill was considered to be magical. These were the Ninja warriors of darkness; assassins of the night. The very name Ninja would terrify people, and they were feared throughout the land. For 400 years the warrior priests who lived with their families in the desolate area in the mountains studied the Buddhist philosophies and secret knowledge of Mikkyo. Mikkyo was the occult teachings and practices of a Buddhist sect known as Shingor, meaning 'true words'. This teaching included the worship of nature spirits, mystic teachings, and Tantric beliefs. Through the study of Tantrism (Hindu writings of a mystical and occult nature) yoga systems were learned, and a method devised to enable the priests to concentrate all of their energy into one endeavour at a time. This involved hand signs of intricate finger-knitting patterns, enabling them to move into a trance-like state. Eventually following the finger-knitting practice, a physiological change would take place, including a slowing down of the blood pressure and heart beat.

The experienced Ninja after learning this art, could shallow breathe, to enable him to feign his own death.

The Ninja's training commenced at birth, and by the age of 5 years he would have learned the 'five exercises' – balance, agility, strength, stamina and special skills. His training would already have begun with the various weapons used by the Ninja. By the age of 7 years, a Ninja child would have learned to hold his breath under water for long periods of time, endure inclement weather, climb trees, scale cliff-faces and walls, and survive for days without food or drink. He would also learn how to sleep on a tree branch without falling off, and be able to dislocate his limbs at will. This limb dislocation would enable him to escape from being bound when tied with ropes or chains. He was also trained psychologically and studied the psychology of human beings, so that when he was acting as a spy or assassin he could use flattery and deception to boost people's egos. He used his understanding of human nature as a deadly weapon.

Stamina was an essential part of the training programme, and so long-distance running was a compulsory exercise. A distance of two or three miles was run as fast as possible to enable a fully trained Ninja to carry messages at a great speed. Month after month the same distance was run, and then the distance would be increased until a distance of fifty miles could be covered at speed.

Some of the training would appear to untrained exponents to be very cruel, as trainees would have to hang from a branch for hours on end to strengthen muscles, and increase mental endurance by going beyond the pain barrier. To be able to enter through small windows and to aid release, they had to utilise the dislocation of joints. These abilities gained the Ninja superhuman status among the people who believed they had special powers.

The stories are many and varied of Ninja who could not be traced because they easily adopted different identities and lived in various homes in different areas.

The costume of the Ninja is called a shinobi shozoku. This consists of a jacket, trousers, hood and split-toed shoes, all in black. The shoes are called tabi and are made of very flexible and pliable leather to enable the Ninja to climb walls, pipes, and fortifications by gripping with the split toe.

At the moment there is apparently a tremendous interest in the Ninja in the USA. Until recently I did not think one could follow Ninja training as it was not only so difficult, but took a lifetime to learn, but I have seen an advertisement for classes in this art. Exactly how much of the art can be taught in a class I do not know, but I do know that the books on Ninja were removed from the library because some of its methods were being used in gang warfare.

The sad fact is, that some of the Ninja weaponry has been copied and is on sale in certain places and outlets. This has increased the violence of street fighting in this country, and this is one of the dangers of teaching the Martial Arts. They were never intended to terrorise people generally, but were designed to be used in warfare conditions. Today with so much violence on the screen and in books, the use of these fighting techniques has become common usage amongst criminally intentioned sections of the public.

The Samurai

As some of the Samurai fighting methods have been incorporated in the Martial Arts I feel it is necessary to write a few details of who they were. The clan chieftains who were called 'daimyos', commanded groups of armed retainers who were called 'The Samurai'. These Samurai were bound in loyalty to their chieftain by the very strictest code of honour, but they were completely ruthless and treated the peasants in the most inhuman way.

Towards the end of the 16th century AD one clan, called 'Tokugawa' made themselves head over all of the

Samurai clans. These men were known as Shogun, and the chieftain of this clan was known as 'The Shogun'. He was in fact the Commander-in-Chief of all fuedal Japan. The Shogun desired to keep the common people under his complete control, and when the Catholic missionaries arrived in Japan with the desire to convert the people to Christianity, the Shogun decided to completely block any non-Japanese from entering the country. At this time many foreigners were massacred when they tried to come into Japan, and even some Japanese returning to their own country were beheaded. Eventually with the arrival of an American expedition in 1853, the Samurai were disbanded.

The way of the Samurai who were an extremely warlike and ruthless group, who had great pride in themselves and demanded almost god-like status among the population, has lived on through the Martial Arts, especially in certain styles such as shotokan (the Japanese school of Karate), and Kempo. Kendo is another Japanese Martial Art that has a strong influence from the Samurai. The Arts that still use weaponry can be seen to have a more war-like approach to fighting, and have a stronger link with the Samurai.

The fact that a feudal system of domination and control continues to live on today in these Martial Arts, is not fully understood, but the influence of 'The Shogun' and the Samurai lives on through the Martial Arts. If one was to refer to a scripture that personified the outlook of 'The Shogun' it would be difficult to refer to a more suitable passage than Jeremiah 5:26&27:

> *'For among my people are found wicked men;*
> *They lie in wait as one who sets snares;*
> *They set a trap,*
> *They catch men.*
> *As a cage is full of birds,*
> *So their houses are full of deceit.*
> *Therefore they have become great and grown rich.'*

Chapter 7

Religions of the Martial Arts

Introduction

The various philosophical and religious backgrounds of the Martial Arts is such that they have an influence on the whole of the practice of, and participation in, these arts. Every part of the Martial Arts comes from a background of an Eastern religion, and the influence of these religions permeates every part of these arts from the moment a student enters the 'dojo'. The ordered behaviour, the moves, the bowing, all of the mind control, acknowledgement of the 'sensai' (teachers) and shrine, the attitudes, uniforms, and the fighting bouts can be traced back to these religions.

The following information will confirm to Christians just how counter-productive these practices are, and that they are against all the teaching in the Bible. To fully understand all that the Martial Arts represent, it is necessary to give some details of the Eastern religions that form such an important part of the Arts. I invite the reader to a brief look at the background and belief system of these religions.

In some instances the whole teaching and practice of the religion is to quell any reaction to outside stimulus, and a withdrawal into a false world of non-involvement which originally stems from Hinduism. The particular teaching in Buddhism and Zen Buddhism is to withdraw into oneself, and this is paricularly emphasised in the self-improvement techniques. Both Buddhism and Zen Buddhism have roots in Hinduism. These attitudes become clearer as the student moves upwards through the grades, and involved in these attitudes of perfection is also a fear of not placating the gods, and their subsequent anger and retribution.

In some of these religions there is a particular emphasis on the sanctity of all life, for in their belief in reincarnation there is the possibility when one is reborn, that one may come back as an animal or insect. Indeed, according to one's Karma, the process could reverse from an animal or insect into a human being. This explains why there is a vegetarian diet, for the thought of eating a relative is unacceptable.

Where a vegetarian diet is recommended or indeed prescribed, it will almost certainly involve following a pattern of vegetarianism in keeping with a particular belief system. So it can be seen how a student may become more and more involved with the following of an Eastern religious discipline.

There is a similarity in the Martial Arts to other organised groups where the full knowledge of all that that group represents is only known as one advances through the levels and grades. It is only then that an awareness of the full details become gradually clearer, and a deeper understanding is gained. By that time it is more difficult to extricate oneself from further involvement. This knowledge comes as the student is assessed for his behaviour, mind control, ability and reliability. When the sensai agree the student is ready he will then be moved on to another grade.

One can now see why it is such a pity that parents in particular allow their children to join these classes thinking that the exercises will do them good, when the truth is that there is a strong possibility that the children may be affected mentally and spiritually by such an introduction to the Martial Arts. Parents are given children by God Almighty, and they are entrusted into their care to guide and lead them in righteous living, I find it very sad that so many parents today have so little concern or understanding of the areas that mean potential danger to their children.

Shintoism

Shinto is the national religion of Japan although it does not have a central system of beliefs as most other religions have. Shintoism pre-dates prehistoric times and means 'the way of the spirits'. It is a practical belief in many gods and goddesses, and many lords, and includes one very important and central god – the sun-goddess Amaterasu. The religion comes from an oral tradition which believes that the islands of Japan were the first divine creation. The most sacred place in Japan is the shrine dedicated to Amaterasu 200 miles south west of Tokyo. The origins of worshipping at this shrine pre-date the time of Christ.

That the main deity of Shinto is feminine rather than masculine is unique among world religions. Also unique is the fact that Shinto is particularly a Japanese religion and it encompasses a love of Japan with the Japanese believing that Japan is a superior nation. This national idealism and confidence of the divinity of Japan is still a part of the Japanese today.

A Shinto scholar of the period of Hirata wrote:

'The Mikado is the true son of heaven who is entitled to reign over the four seas and the ten thousand countries.'

This led to an acceptance amongst the people that their ruler is in fact divine, and although in recent times this has been discouraged, the Emperor still finds the people expect him to attend certain imperialistic duties involving Shinto celebrations.

The central belief of the state is that Shinto is the divine spirit in all of nature which is thought of in feminine terms. The Japanese conclude that since all human beings are the offspring of nature, whatever they think or do must be natural and therefore right. The consequence of this is that they believe there is no such thing as wickedness in the sight of God. Whatever is, is right, and mankind stands in no need of redemption. This was a very useful belief for unscrupulous leaders and was readily accepted by the people as an excellent idea. This belief was taught in many of the schools.

Included in the Shinto belief alongside the many gods and goddesses, are several animal and female demons who come to torment any that displease them. Therefore one can see why it is necessary to placate the Kami who are accepted as being very superior beings, and represent the sacred power found in all things. It is believed that the Japanese people descend from the Kami, but the Emperor descends from Amaterusa. Also as a part of placating the gods, the priests sell a profitable line of lucky charms freely purchased by the people to protect them from the gods and demons.

There is an enormous amount of pride and feeling of superiority among the Japanese people, and all things of Japanese origin are considered to be of a higher quality than anything from any other source. This feeling of pride gives a degree of confidence to its populace and is totally against all that Christianity teaches. In fact the Bible teaches the very opposite to pride, as the teaching of our God is to prefer the other person, and to remember that God made man, so we have no right to consider ourselves better than others. The following passages make this matter quite clear:

> 'Pride goes before destruction,
> a haughty spirit before a fall.

> *Better to be lowly in spirit and among the oppressed*
> *than to share plunder with the proud.'*
>
> (Proverbs 16:18&19 NIV)

> *'Do nothing out of selfish ambition or vain conceit, but*
> *in humility consider others better than yourselves. Each*
> *of you should look not only to your own interests, but*
> *also to the interests of others.'*
>
> (Philippians 2:3&4 NIV)

The background story to Shintoism as told in the 'Ko-ji-ki', is that the earliest of the celestial gods instructed two other gods, Izanagi and Izanami who were both male and female, to create the world through sexual regeneration, whereupon they together produced all of nature, the land, the Kami, mountains, streams etc.

There are no particular sacred books to Shintoism as in other religions, but books that are considered of great importance are the Ko-ji-ki which contains details of ancient matters, and Nihongi, a book recording the history of Japan. This book chronicles the birth of Japan and was compiled from around 720 BC until 700 BC. The Ko-ji-ki contains an assortment of historical myths and legend.

The people who follow the way of Shinto, have shrines in their own homes, and all of life is governed by their belief. Their local shrine will be of great importance and will be visited on a regular basis. Everything they do will be influenced by the belief of the power of the gods.

One instance of this effect on all things in life by the Shintoism religion is found in the potters craft centre. When the time comes for firing the pottery, a ceremony takes place to ensure the successful outcome of the firing, and to make sure that no pots will be cracked or broken or marred in any way. Salt is shaken all around the whole area of the kiln which takes days to prepare for firing. Prayers are said, and saki (an alcoholic drink) is poured on the ground and around the firing area. No matter that all other areas of the pottery may be built in a modern setting and surrounded by expensive houses filled with the latest technology, the ancient rites still have a great and important meaning for the inhabitants.

Following the Second World War the Shinto state was abolished as the religion of the people, but the shrines and priests are still supported financially by the people, and all family ceremonies will be led by a Shinto priest who is paid for his duties. The Shinto belief is still very much alive and the gods and goddesses are still worshipped.

As we have already seen, Shinto is part of all Sumo wrestling bouts, and the influence of Shinto underlines all the Japanese Martial Arts. The bowing at the start of a practice or competition comes from the Japanese and Shintoism. Any shrine or other article of reverence in the dojo, is part of Shintoism. Nippon also covers every Martial Art originating in Japan. The continuing faith of Shinto despite the abolition nationally of this faith, has made little difference to the majority of the Japanese, because this faith is built on fear, and there is an undercurrent of fear that holds those still following this faith to continue appeasing the gods.

The vegetarian diet of many of the Eastern religions is connected with their view of re-incarnation. The Christian faith has no such belief as we are promised a place in Heaven when we die (John 3:15 and John 6:47). Both these verses tell of how those who believe in Christ and follow His ways will have life everlasting. In Acts 11:10, we can read the story concerning Peter when he had a vision from God of a sheet being let down full of four-footed animals, wild beasts, creeping things, and birds of the air, and a voice which told him to arise *'kill and eat'*, and Peter refused saying that nothing unclean had entered his mouth. The voice said, *'What God has cleansed you must not call common'* and this was repeated three times. This command from God proves that the creation of animals, fish, birds, and insects were all for the care and use of man, as has already been referred to. Genesis

1:26–31 confirms this fact, and as the word in Acts shows, it was God's plan that man should subdue the creatures of the land and use them for his benefit.

Hinduism

Hinduism is one of the oldest religions in the world, and the Hindu scriptures were written over a period of 2,000 years, from 1400 BC to 500 AD. These scriptures are extremely complex and varied, and they divide into categories; Scruti, that ... that has been heard, and Smriti, that ... that has been remembered.

There are many different sects and divisions in Hinduism which vary from one community to another. One sect that is well known is ISKON, which stands for, International Society for Krishna Consciousness; the Hare Krishna cult.

As Hinduism grew, various groups added other elements into their ceremonies which included new ways towards reaching perfection. This state of perfection is named Nirvana. Nirvana can also be found in Buddhism which is an offshoot of Hinduism. Nirvana is the Hindu concept of complete happiness, and final fulfilment. The recorded truths of Hinduism are contained in many books. The Vedas contain the wisdom, and cover several books. The contents include the mantras which are hymns of praise to the gods Brahmanas, the teaching of ritual rights, and the Rig-veda hymns and praises to the Hindu deities, Indra, Soma, Varuna, and Mitra.

The Upanishads deal with religious truths and doctrine. Another of the Vedas is called Athara-Veda, this is a book of magic spells and incantations to be performed by the priests. Various other books are Ramayana, one of two epic tales, and the Mahabharata. Both of these tales are still enacted today; the Mahabharata has recently been serialised on TV and it lasted for 64 episodes.

The most sacred book in the Hindu faith is the Bhagavad-Gita, which is also the best known of all the

Hindu writings. The Bhagavad-Gita means 'The song of the lord', and it speaks of lord Krishna who was the incarnation of the Hindu god Vishnu. In these scriptures it says that even those who worship other gods with love and sacrifice, in fact really worship the same gods as the Hindus. This belief can also be found in the New Age movement where it does not matter who or what you worship; all are accepted.

In fact this attitude is creeping into liberal Christianity which not only weakens the teachings of Christ, but plays straight into the hands of the enemy.

Krishna is considered to be the central god of the Hindus, and is called Brahman, the supreme spirit, the ultimate reality. The three main spirits of Brahman are:
- Brahma, Lord of creation.
- Vishnu, the preserver, appearing as Rama and Krishna.
- Shiva, who represents power and destruction.

There is no single Hindu idea of god. There are many beliefs which may include any of the following concepts:
- Shiva god of song and healing.
- Durga divine goddess of motherhood.
- Vishnu god of space and time.

The common belief is that Brahman is the one god over Brahma the creator, Vishnu the preserver and Shiva the destroyer; these three are in one god.

Reincarnation is known as Karma, that we are all accountable for our own actions, and that bad actions must be atoned for through the Samsara, or reincarnation. How one has lived one's life on earth, determines the life to come through reincarnation; whether that life is to be lived in the body of an animal, human being, insect, plant or inanimate object. The Hindus see reincarnation in this way:

> As a man casts off his worn out clothes and takes on other new ones in their place, so does the embodied soul cast off his worn out body and enters a new one.

Brahman, the Hindus believe, exists in everything; all parts of nature and every living thing including man. At the heart of this faith is a great reverence for life. We can see why, when we understand their belief in reincarnation, and why they believe all living things whether animal or human should be seen to be treasured and loved. This leads to an avoidance of killing any living creature, and gives a foundation for their vegetarianism.

They believe that as Brahma is in all things, that animals have souls. The cow has a special place, in that it is revered, and believed to have great power. Here are a few extracts from a long poem written in praise of the cow:

> Worship to thee, springing to life,
>   and worship to thee when born,
> Worship, O cow to thy tail hair,
>   and to thy hooves and to thy form.
>
> They call the cow immortal life,
>   pay homage to the cow as death.
> She hath become this universe,
>   Fathers and Rishis hath become the gods,
> and men the spirits.
>
> The cow is heaven, the cow is earth,
>   the cow is Vishnu Lord of life.
>
> Both gods and mortal men depend for life
>   and being on the cow.
> She hath become this universe;
>   all that the sun surveys is she.
>
> (Atharva Veda X:10)

The only way for Hindus to be free from reincarnation is by Moksha. This is perfect peace and happiness. To attain this goal the soul has to be completely free from any and every feeling of desire or attachment. The aids to this are, meditation, knowledge, and a lack of selfishness or a grudge against anybody. This is considered to be god-centred.

The four main stages in life lead one towards a state of Moksha and they are as follows:
1.   Childhood and schooling.
2.   Marriage and family.
3.   The time after the children have left home.
4.   Life of the recluse or world renouncer.

Stage 1

A young person is expected to concentrate his mind and energies on completing this first stage of schooling and study before passing on to the next stage.

Stage 2

This is the time for a young person to become married and raise a family. At this time his life is one of building the family unit and raising his children in the true faith of Hinduism.

Stage 3

This is a time of rediscovering his own place in the world, and his relationship with his wife, and eventually his grandchildren.

Stage 4

At this stage one has normally retired from one's everyday occupation and one's mind concentrates on reaching Moksha.

Some Hindus leave home at this time and travel to a holy place where they can meditate in their quest for Moksha or Mukti, to enable them to find release from the cycle of birth and rebirth, and death, known as Samsara. A pilgrimage is considered of great importance towards gaining Moksha, and one of the holy places to visit is the river Ganges. To have visited this river before one dies is thought to be a great blessing, and is the desired place to visit by all Hindus.

The caste system is a unique part of the Hindu faith, and even though this system has been decried by the Government it is still very much in existence. This caste system accepts the belief that there are various classes of people:

 - The **Brahmins**, who are the priests and philosophers and are subsidised by the state.
 - The **Kshatriyas**, who are the upper middle classes.
 - The **Vaisyas**, who are merchants and farmers.
 - The **Sudras**, who are the lowest of the caste system and whose job it is to serve the higher classes as labourers and servants. They are excluded from any religious service and are not allowed to study the sacred writings of the Vedas.

There are several other sub-classes besides these mentioned. The caste system affects every part of life, and even the Christian churches are affected by this system as the people who attend the churches are mainly from one particular caste. The dowry tradition is still in a place of importance, and when a young girl marries, her father will demand a dowry from the husband to be according to the father's status. This can be a matter of continual contention if the girl's husband has a problem repaying the father. The caste system is a difficult problem, especially for Christians who teach God's Word that all people are equal. 1 Corinthians 12:7–31 contains the description of how we are all one, but to each is given a different talent for the good of all. Not that one is better than another but as each receives a gift that is used for the Lord, so all thing work together.

Another tradition that is still kept alive within the Hindu faith is the tradition of taking offerings to the temples for the various gods and goddesses; gifts of flowers, food, leaves, water, and other love gifts. Where there aren't any statues, gifts will be placed before a picture of the chosen god or goddess. Besides taking offerings to the temples, quite often there is a family shrine within the household. This will be a favourite god or goddess, and it will be venerated as the protector of the house and family.

Every morning a ceremony is carried out. This ceremony is called 'Waking the deity'. A lamp fed with ghee (which is clarified butter) is placed before the statue or picture, and then some food is put there. Prayers will be spoken, and after this, the statue is bathed with a mixture of yoghurt, honey, milk and sugar, some ghee is added and stirred together. Following this, the statue is dressed with flowers, sandalwood, paste, turmeric, and red kumkum powder.

Incense is burned and a bell summons and proclaims the presence of the deity. Then the ghee lamp is lit and moved in a circle before the face of the god. This offering of light is called 'Arti'. All present receive the lamp and pass their hands over the flame and lift their hands over their face and hair. The daily prayer is then said, which is called 'Gayatri Mantra'. At meals a portion of the food is offered at the shrine before returning the food to the table, the food then becomes 'Parshad'; that is blessed.

The worship of an inanimate object could not be farther from the teachings of Christ. The Bible clearly states there is only one god, and that is the Lord God Almighty who created the heavens and the earth, and for Christians to be involved with this Indian religion includes the participants in a multi-god faith. All the moves are based on the Hindu worship of all creatures, and on the movements of the animals and birds etc. The outcome of involvement with the Martial Arts with a Hindu background, can be and often is, confusion.

Buddhism

Although Buddhist origins are from Hinduism in India, its influence has now spread to most continents in the world including China, Japan, and Europe. Its accepted founder Siddhartha Guatama was born in 560 BC in Nepal on the Northern frontier of India. The records of Siddhartha Guatama's life and beliefs were collected 300 years after his death, and have been included in the Sanskrit accounts, which are the classical Hindu scriptures. The inspiration of his life is still evident today, and whether some of the details are myth or truth is of little importance to Buddhist followers.

Guatama was born into a Royal family, his father being the King Suddhodana. As his father had known the suffering of the world, he wanted to protect his son from all human misery. Therefore, orders were issued to all members of the staff and household that Guatama was to be kept from seeing any of the suffering, misery, and evil of the world, and he was to be kept within the confines of the Palace and its grounds. Nevertheless, Guatama escaped to the city one day, and there he witnessed all that his father had tried so hard to protect him from. For the first time he saw cripples begging, disease and death. He was so affected by these things that he determined to spend the rest of his life on a pilgrimage of asceticism and enquiry.

Guatama had been raised as a Hindu, but during his search for an answer to the suffering of mankind he gradually became disillusioned with the Hindu faith. For seven days Guatama sat under a fig tree meditating, and such was his meditation that it is believed that he reached the highest degree of god-consciousness, which became known as the state of Nirvana. After achieving this state he was no longer known as Siddhartha Guatama but Buddha, 'The Enlightened One'.

Guatama named four noble truths whilst he was meditating under the fig tree, and these became a basic part of Buddhism which he determined to teach to Buddhist followers. The fig tree was ever after known as the 'tree of wisdom' and called 'Bodhi' or the 'Lo' tree.

Contrary to most of the world religions, Guatama believed that to have numerous gods and goddesses was futile. The fact that he was disillusioned with Hinduism must have led him to believe the worship of these things did not result in the desired result. His aim was to initiate a belief system for all men, and not just for the priests and nuns. This belief system was based on kindness to others, including animals, and a respect for all life of every type and kind. This truth he believed would bring peace and happiness to the individual, and alleviate any worry and concern over himself, his family, and his future.

Guatama taught that as most of life is full of unhappiness and tension, it causes people to desire the wrong things. He taught that stilling the mind and discovering contentment by meditation and discipline would bring complete happiness; a state of Nirvana.

The ultimate desire of Buddhists is to become good enough to reach a state of Nirvana. This state is similar to reaching sainthood, but the Buddhist passes through many lives on his continuous improvement pilgrimage, re-incarnating after death, hopefully with a chance of a better life.

The unfortunate women can't possibly reach a level nearer to Nirvana until they re-incarnate as a man, as no female can reach the desired state of perfection and pleasure of Nirvana as a female.

The Indian people were disillusioned with Hinduism and so eagerly listened to the teachings Buddha laid down. The following are 'The Middle Path' – the noble path that leads to the cessation of pain. By the time of Buddha's death at the age of eighty, these teachings had become a strong force in India.

The Four Noble Truths

1st Noble Truth
Life is full of sorrow, birth is painful, death is painful, disease and old age are painful. Both having what we desire is painful, and not having what we desire is painful.

2nd Noble Truth
This concerns the cause of suffering. It is the craving desire for the pleasures of the senses which seeks satisfaction now here, now there, the craving for happiness and prosperity in this life and future lives.

3rd Noble Truth
To end suffering one needs to give up any craving, passion or desire. Until this aim is achieved, suffering will continue.

4th Noble Truth
To end all pain, one must follow the Eight-Fold Path.

'*The First Step*' is to follow the teachings on this Eight-Fold Path with 'Right Views'. You must accept the Four Noble Truths and the Eight-Fold Path.

'*The Second Step*' is 'Right Resolve'. You must renounce the pleasures of the senses; you must harbour no ill-will toward anyone and harm no living creature.

'*The Third Step*' is 'Right Speech'. Do not lie, do not slander or abuse anyone. Do not indulge in idle talk.

'*The Fourth Step*' is 'Right Behaviour'. Do not destroy any living creature; take only what is given you; do not commit any unlawful sexual act.

'*The Fifth Step*' is 'Right Occupation'. You must earn your livelihood in a way that will harm no-one.

'*The Sixth Step*' is 'Right Effort'. You must resolve and strive heroically to prevent any evil qualities from arising in you and to abandon any evil qualities that you may possess. You must grow, increase and be perfected.

'*The Seventh Step*' is 'Right Contemplation'. Be observant, strenuous, alert, contemplative, free from desire and of sorrow.

'*The Eighth Step*' is 'Right Meditation'. When you have abandoned all sensuous pleasures, all evil qualitites, both joy and sorrow, you must then enter the four degrees of meditation, which are produced by concentration.

Buddhist Precepts
There are five precepts taught by Buddhism that all Buddhists should follow:
1. Kill no living thing, including insects.
2. Do not steal.
3. Do not commit adultery.

4. Tell no lies.
5. Do not take any intoxicating drinks, or drugs.
There are some other precepts but they are only for monks and nuns.

Zen Buddhism

Zen Buddhism is a branch of Buddhism that has spread to the West and is well known by name if not in detail. The origins of Zen have been attributed to the monk Bodhidharma who originated from India. It is said that he believed that a thought transferance could take place from one person to another purely by concentrated thought, and so by-passing any verbal communication. Bodhidharma's explanation to the Emperor at that time was this:

– A special tradition outside of the scriptures.
– No dependence on words.
– A direct pointing at man.
– Seeing into one's own nature, and the attainment of wisdom.

Although the development of Zen was a long time after the death of Buddha, it still maintained the important teachings on meditation. This precept of meditation was what originally led the Buddha towards enlightenment. 'Self-Effort' is the basis of Zen practice, with an emphasis on concentration leading to enlightenment. This enlightenment is called 'Satori'.

The daily practice of sitting cross-legged in either the half lotus position, or full lotus position where the legs are crossed with the feet being brought up to the surface beside the knees, is practised for long intensive periods and is called 'Zazen'. The chanting of a Sutra may also accompany the meditation. A Sutra consists of an extract from Sanskrit literature.

A Koan will be given to the student for him to consider, it is believed this solving of a Koan will lead the student towards enlightenment. An instance of a Koan is:

We are all familiar with two hands clapping, what is the sound of one hand? (If you protest that one hand can't clap, you go to the foot of the class. Such a remark simply shows that you haven't even begun to get the point.)

The study and meditation in Zen eventually leads the student to a state where there is a lack of logical thinking, and the student will lose all his critical faculties. This attitude leads towards a withdrawal from life. With the student reaching this state it makes it particularly difficult to witness with any success to a Buddhist, as his mind and feelings appear to be so far away that one cannot make contact on a normal level. The aim of Zen would appear to be the practice of losing one's own sense of evaluation and logical thinking, and retreat into a world of living without natural feeling.

The Christian concept of living in the world is so different from the attitude of Zen Buddhism, as the foundation of the Christian faith is love, and to love one has to be able to feel and recognise different emotions. The Zen Buddhist teaching is to reach a place where one is no longer aware of feelings; neither love nor hate. Jesus' words in John 15:9–13 all speak of Jesus' love for us, and that He laid down His life for us. Love is the central teaching in Christianity, but I have yet to find any mention or teaching of love in these Eastern religions.

Confucianism

Confucianism has a strong tradition in China, and it so affects the people's thinking and attitudes, that it is important for something to be written concerning this subject.

Confucianism is more a philosophy than a religion; a way of relating to, and integrating with, the world and man-to-man; and advice on ways of relating to the almighty. This philosophy still has a strong influence on the way the Chinese people's faith in Taoism and their thoughts, morals, and actions are affected.

Confucius was born in about 550 BC in Shantung China. After having been married and producing a son and daughter, he was divorced. As a teacher, reputation for his wisdom spread, and he became a teacher of some note, especially in the realm of political and social reforms. He spent his last years writing what have become Confucianist classics. Confucius' impact on Chinese thought was enormous, and in 206 BC Confucianism became the State religion. Even so, in 212 BC Emperor Shi Huang Ti ordered all books on Confucianism to be burned, and established Taoism in its place, but this did not have the desired effect, and the following Emperors all accepted Confucianism, and sacrificed at his tomb.

By 574 to 581 AD Emperor Wu announced that in his opinion Confucianism should be the people's first choice, with Taoism second and Buddhism third. Following this order concerning the religions in China, different Emperors from 841–847 AD issued varying orders, including the closing of the Monasteries and Nunneries, but despite these events the people's loyalty to these faiths have continued up to today, and they are very much alive and practised regularly.

In 1068 AD Confucius was raised to the rank of Emperor, and in 1906 he was raised to the rank of co-assessor with the deities of Heaven and Earth.

The teachings of Confucius are mostly concerning morals and the way to live. Among these teachings there is one called 'Filial Piety' which concerns devotion and obedience by the younger members of a family to the elders, particularly in the case of a father and son. This devotion is demonstrated while the parents are alive, and shown after their death with grief and sorrow. The outworking of this teaching is that Chinese families look after their parents, if necessary in their own homes until these parents die. This teaching has also underlined the fact that on entering a home, one first makes obeisance to the family shrine, which will mostly be one of photos and memorabilia placed on a sideboard or table just inside the front door. This veneration of the ancestors is a difficult situation for Chinese Christians, as the ancestors are not released in any way for a new life after death, as we Christians believe.

Amongst the 'Ethical Doctrines' are many virtuous edicts that are good, but one of these edicts displays the difference in this philosophy and the Christian faith:

> We know so little about life, how can we then know about death?

Although many of these teachings of Confucius seem good advice, they differ from Christ's teachings in several ways. One way is this; that all the teaching is about self-effort, while the teaching in Christianity is that man hasn't the ability to save himself without the help of a saviour. The emphasis of Confucius' teaching is of the intellect, and says nothing of the supernatural. It appears to be a man-made explanation of ways to exist in the world with one's fellow-man.

Taoism

Taoism is perhaps the most difficult religion to understand. For those brought up in the West it might appear almost incomprehensible, as it is as much a philosophy as a religion. Its aims are to deepen and expand the mind. Taoism is based more on a variety of thoughts and ideas that have gradually evolved into a way of life, than a religion with a central deity. The basic structure of belief is not based on any belief that the world was created by any being of any kind, whether a god or human. The following extract may help to clarify the matter.

> 'But let us ask whether there is a creator or not. If not, how can he create things? If there is, he is

capable of materializing all forms. Therefore before we can talk about creation we must understand the fact that all forms materialize by themselves. If we go through the entire realm of existence, we shall see there is nothing, not even penumbra that does not transform itself beyond the phenomenal world. Hence everything creates itself without the direction of any creator. Since things create themselves they are unconditioned. This is the norm of the universe.'

(Commentary of Chuang Tzu sec 2:2, 46–47
Sources of Chinese tradition from Kuo Hsiang,
a commentator of the 3rd, to 4th century)

The origins of the philosophy and religion of Taoism arose out of a Shamanistic belief which is believed to be one of the oldest religions.

It has been claimed, and is believed that the original creator of Taoism was a man named Lao-tzu who was born in 604–570 BC. He disapproved of the way the rulers in China dominated and cruelly treated the people under their rule. Some people claim this man never lived, but whether the legend of Lao-tzu is true or not, it is claimed that he wrote a book called *The Tao Te King* also known as *Lao-tzu*. This book contained instructions for a leadership of non-action and less governmental control. Although it would seem the rulers did not put this suggestion into action, the philosophy contained in this book had, and still has a tremendous following in China. The advice to the common people was to withdraw from any ambition because of the harsh and cruel rule in the country at that time, and also to withdraw from any emotional involvement. This was to try and help the populace to survive with as little turmoil in their lives as possible, and to also survive physically. This attitude of a mental non-action still lives on today, and has an overall effect on people's view of life.

This teaching, and the fact that Taoism as such has no writings on how to survive evil other than by escaping mentally, could not be further from the teachings of Christ. God sent His only Son into the world to live and work among His people, to teach them how to **live** life – not how to **ignore** life. Christ was involved with all that was of the world and the people, and His words were very much concerned with how to cope with evil in this world. Jesus Christ's ministry was very much about involvement and action. He healed the sick, He delivered those who were affected by evil spirits, He taught the people, and He was very interested in the lives of people on earth. How different this is from the Taoist teaching, where there is no caring for others, no loving, no helping others, no concern for others, but only, a concern of how to get through life oneself; a very self-centred religion.

Taoism was established in 212 BC by the then Emperor Shi Huang. The basic belief was that there were two worlds existing side by side; nature and spiritual beings overlapping but distinct from the physical world and the spirit world. This spirit world includes all things of nature; trees, streams, animals, earth, plants, rocks, and each has a spirit; therefore we must care for these things or we may be affected in an undesirable way.

The Shaman has an important and central part of all things in Taoism, as it is believed he is able to make contact with the spirit world, and in a trance state is enabled to speak through the spirits. His power is such that he will be consulted in cases of hardship or illness to discover what offence has been commited to cause the undesired situation. This attitude of fear causes people to treat all nature with great respect. The word Shaman comes from Siberia and spread to China across to Japan into South East Asia, across to Alaska and down the length of North and Central America. As this belief system grew it eventually became known as Taoism (Tao = path or way).

Yin and Yang are important to Taoists and they believe that through combining the two forces and powers, renewal will come. Thus when the weather is mostly Yin (deep winter), that is the point at which nature moves towards spring and summer (Yang).

A book called *Tao Ta Ching* has had a profound effect on the final outcome of Taoism which embraced a desire for immortality. This involved several searches including the consumption of imperishable material such as jade, gold etc. and herbs and magical prescriptions. This search for immortality continued for a considerable length of time with little effect. In fact, sometimes instead of lengthening the span of years, a life was cut short by the consumption of these materials, some of which were poisonous.

It is interesting to consider the fact that there are still groups of people in the world today, searching and claiming ways of attaining immortality. But for Christians, although we desire to live the number of our days fit and well, we have no need to search for immortality, as this life on earth is only the precursor of a life in Heaven, where death and sickness will be no more.

Christ said:

> '*I tell you the truth, whoever hears my word and believes him who sent me has eternal life and will not be condemned, he has crossed over from death to life.*'
>
> (John 5:24 NIV)

This passage in Jesus Christ's own words gives the truth of a life to come for all who believe in Him.

In AD 471 the first cannon of scripture was compiled and Taoist monks and priests were initiated. They lived, and still do, by charging for their services at weddings, funerals, festivals, etc. and they have a scale of charges that has enabled them to still be operative today.

One path of inner transformation is through purification, and the correct breathing called 'chi', There are many types of breath. One is called 'embryonic breath' and this is considered to be of great importance. Exercises were also developed to enable the body to relax and be in balance, Tai Chi is one such discipline.

Taoism is still very much alive today, and a Taoist family will see that an offering is made to the Earth god of the house or the flat first thing in the morning. Maybe joss sticks will be lit with an offering of prayer, and tea or cakes placed before the god. This god will be a totally Taoist deity; he or she will represent the primal force or deity that inhabits the dwelling place, and is called 'The house god'. All activities have to be planned with the permission of this house god. As the Taoist faith has developed, so the number of gods have grown, and the following is a guide to some of the better known gods.

Heavenly Sage – Jade Emperor – Jade dawn of the golden gate, who has the elements of the future and of the way about him. The jade emperor has forces to help him to ensure obedience to his will. *Erh-ling* – his nephew. Erhling is the most powerful of all the Taoist gods. Erh-ling carries out the orders and commands of the Jade Emperor who presides over ministries of: thunder, wind, wealth, literature, war, exorcism, and illness.

Wang – his door keeper.

Earthly Hierachy – over earth and water, water dragon kings and their hordes, with four dragon kings.

Earth Great Emperor of the Eastern Peak (a holy mountain) – gods of the walls and ditches report back to the great Emperor as to whether the people are keeping their side of the balance of Yin and Yang.

Two door gods: **Wealth** – Tsa'ai Shen, god of literature; **Kuan Ti** – god of war and his two companions.

Emperess of Heaven – goddess of the seas.

Ten Kings of Hell – **King Yama** the head. He is pictured on all the banks of hell notes which are burned every day to appease the gods and provide a means to live for the dead.

- **1st Hell**: King Ch'in Kuang
- **2nd Hell**: Chi-chiang
- **3rd Hell**: Sung-ti
- **4th Hell**: King Wu-Kuan
- **5th Hell**: King Yama

- **6th Hell**: King Pien ch'eng
- **7th Hell**: King T'ai-shan Chun
- **8th Hell**: King Ping-teng
- **9th Hell**: King Tu-shih
- **10th Hell**: King Chuan-lun in charge of the wheel of rebirth.

Three Gods of Happiness – these are found in all places, especially in the temple in Kowloon, and they include: longevity, happiness and success.

The priest's main emphasis is to continue the cycle of cosmic renewal liturgies, and the balance of Yin and Yang.

> Give way and overcome
> Bend and become straight
> Empty yourself and be full
> Use up things and they are new.
>
> (Tas Te Ching Ch.22)

> Which is more important?
> Your fame or your true self?
> Your true self or your wealth?
> Which is ultimately more valuable?
>
> (Tas Te Ching Ch.44)

The previous lists of the gods and goddesses is given to show the fear and complexity of Taoism. Life is a continuous process of placating the gods and goddesses for fear of their anger and any possible retribution. This is a very intellectual religion, and has a continual emphasis on the mental approach. The koans for example, are all of the mind, and have no correct answer as far as one can see. This is all so far from the simplicity of the Christian faith, and the teaching and God's words of the world's creation in perfection.

> *'God saw all that He had made, and it was very good.'*
>
> (Genesis 1:31 NIV)

'He waters the mountains from his upper chambers;
  the earth is satisfied by the fruit of his work ...
The moon marks off the seasons,
  and the sun knows when to go down ...
How many are your works O LORD!
  In wisdom you made them all;
  the earth is full of your creatures.'
                                        (Psalm 104:13, 19, 24 NIV)

This is a most wonderful psalm of praise to God for His creation.

Chapter 8

Yoga

Yoga comes from the Sanskrit word 'yuj' meaning to bind, join, attach, and yoke. This implies one has to concentrate one's full attention, and it also means a union, and communion. The ultimate final aim, is to become one with the 'Divine Universal Spirit' Brahma, Paramatmà or god. It is believed that we can all tune in to this universal spirit by attuning our minds, and being free from all in this world that affects our peace of mind, and that through practising Yoga one is able to reach a state of Mokksa or Mukti. This state is considered to lead to a liberation from all earthly sorrow and pain, all desire and anxiety. The true meaning of Yoga embraces a belief in freedom from success or failure.

Yoga embraces many philosophies, including aspects of Greek mythology, the occult, and Hinduism. From Hinduism much of the philosophy is from the most sacred writings of the Bhagavad Gita. This is considered to be the most sacred writing in all of Hindu written works, and was written in the first century AD. Many of the Eastern religions include Yoga as part of the practice of withdrawal from the world and its concerns including Hinduism, Buddhism, and particularly Zen Buddhism. Most of the Martial Art students are recommended the practice of meditation techniques to aid their concentration, and the development of chi or ki power.

The best known of all the stages in the study of Yoga is *Hatha Yoga*. This includes a series of exercises named 'Asanas'. There are fifty-seven different positions, aimed at improving the mind and spirit, so that the whole man may be a fit vehicle for the spirit. Each position represents a part of nature, and the stance will demonstrate the animal, tree, or part of nature it copies. Some of the positions are named as follows:

- **Vrksa**: The tree.
- **Vrschika**: The scorpion.
- **Salabha**: The locust.
- Any of the following – fish, tortoise, frog, crocodile, cock, heron, peacock, swan, dog, horse, camel, lion, serpent, or the human embryonic state.

Besides the Asanas the breathing techniques will be studied, and these are known by the name of:

- **Prànàyàma**: Breathing exercises. These must not be confused with other methods of breathing exercises, as these exercises are accompanied by certain mind and mental procedures.
- **Pratyàhàra**: Most commonly practised, as this is a complete method of withdrawal from the world by controlling one's thoughts and senses. A subject to enable the student to concentrate is given by the teacher. This may be a picture, to teach how to still the mind.
- **Dhyana**: This is the next stage in meditation, and a mantra will more than likely be given, this is repeated over and over again until a state of withdrawal is experienced.

There are other areas in the study of Yoga, and teachers (named gurus) may choose to teach one area before another. These other stages include: advanced asanas, inner cleansing techniques, and other methods of self-improvement. A student will more than likely be advised to follow a vegetarian diet in order to cleanse the body of unwanted substances, and to aid one's spiritual development. They will also be advised to avoid all foods that are: sour, bitter, pungent, tasteless, heavy, or considered by Hindus to be unclean. Perfection for the yogi is to never feel heat or cold, pain or pleasure, honour or dishonour, virtue or vice, disaster or success. It is claimed that when one reaches this state one becomes free from birth, death, pain or sorrow, and becomes immortal. The ultimate end is to become one in the mind with the Divine Universal Spirit that is Brahma. Brahma is the first member of the Hindu triad of Brahma, Shiva, and Vishnu. Brahma is the creator god.

As a yogi (one who studies and practises the way of Yoga) moves on through the various stages, he is endeavouring to reach a state of one-ness with this Universal Spirit, but in so doing he is gradually retreating farther and farther away from the real world into a position similar to a drugged state; into a withdrawal from earthly things. The truth is that as one progresses towards the final 'Samsara' (the end of reincarnation and the final release from a returning to this cycle of rebirth) the enemy is also gradually invading the person through his very passivity of mind. The yogi believes that he is succeeding in his retreat from this world, but his retreat is into a web of the enemy of this world. Ephesians 6:12 speaks clearly of the enemy:

> *'For we do not wrestle against flesh and blood, but against principalities, against powers, against the rulers of the darkness of this age, against spiritual hosts of wickedness in the heavenly places.'*

In Yoga there is no armour, no protection from the enemy. Through the yogi's passivity of mind the enemy has an open door and will take full advantage of this.

There is a Christian way of finding peace with God and oneself, and an emotion of joy and peace far removed from the yogic method of emptying the mind. In 1 Peter 1:13 the advice is the opposite of having a passive mind; it is to stir up the mind:

> *'Therefore prepare your minds for action; be self-controlled; set your hope fully on the grace to be given you when Jesus Christ is revealed.'* (1 Peter 1:13 NIV)

The passages referring to joy and peace are so many that I will just give a few references: Psalms 58:10, 68:3, 107:42, 118:24. To close this section I would like to quote Psalm 33:1–5:

> *Rejoice in the LORD, O you righteous!*
> *For praise from the upright is beautiful.*
> *Praise the LORD with the harp;*
> *Make melody to him with an instrument of ten strings.*
> *Sing to him a new song;*
> *Play skilfully with a shout of joy.*
> *For the word of the LORD is right,*
> *And all his work is done in truth.*
> *He loves righteousness and justice;*
> *The earth is full of goodness of the LORD.*

Chapter 9

Yin and Yang

Yin and Yang are a part of Taoist religion and philosophy. These form a basis and understanding of life and a concept of all things in the ebb and flow of life, and so integrate the gradual changes throughout life thus forming a foundation for a universal principle. Yin and Yang are also a part of the teachings in the Unification Church (the Moonies) where it is called dualism. Father god, Mother god, spirit and flesh, a dual aspect of all things, and is also accepted in the religions of Japan. The term Yin and Yang is from Confucianism and is frequently used today within society. In fact at the moment I have heard people use this term relating to a variety of subjects: cooking, relationships, the weather and emotions; although there doesn't appear to be any understanding of the full meaning of this term.

The two parts of the Yin and Yang sign represent the male and the female. Yin being negative, and Yang positive. Yin is female and Yang male and each side of the sign represents certain features. Yielding and non-action, a natural harmony in all things. The two sides of the sign signify complementary opposites in all creation.

Yin and Yang have a very strong influence in Kung Fu styles. The religion of Taoism is central in these styles of Martial Art, and the Yin and Yang can be seen in the hard and soft styles with their action and non-action.

8 trigrams

Yin – female, dark	**Yang – male, light**
Negative	Positive
Evil	Good
Darkness	Light
Death	Life
Winter	Summer
Passive	Active

Both sides of the symbol are a part of the other, and can only exist together. They are inseparable forces, flowing one into the other. As each flows:

Night into day
Summer into winter
Hard becomes soft
Yin becomes Yang
Yang becomes Yin again.

These symbols of Yin and Yang are surrounded by eight trigrams and all are a part of creation. Each has its own importance and must be in exactly the correct position. First comes Ch'ien which is seen as heaven and creation – three straight lines. Opposite are three broken lines. These represent the earth, K'un. This is passive. The other lines represent lake, fire, thunder, wind, water, and mountains.

One can now see the importance of the Taoist faith on all the Chinese Martial Art styles, and the Yin and Yang which stands for action and non-action. South Korea has this sign on the National flag (their main faith is Buddhism).

Although Yin and Yang originate in Taoism and Confucianism they have a link into all of the Martial Arts through the teaching of Zen Buddhism and the meditation techniques in Buddhism and the practice of Yoga.

The Taoist teaching on Yin and Yang has no foundation in the teaching in the Bible. In Christianity there is no need for a man-made solution towards finding an inward peace and harmony. Christ taught that peace comes with obedience in following the teaching He gave us, and in accepting His love and care for us, and so through His love we can love others. In Yin and Yang there is a male dominance that is ungodly and an attitude that finds no place in the Christian teachings. In Galatians 3:26–28 it says this:

> 'For you are all sons of God through faith in Jesus Christ. For as many of you as were baptised into Christ have put on Christ. There is neither Jew nor Greek, there is neither slave nor free, there is neither male nor female: for you are all one in Jesus Christ.'

Chapter 10

Bowing

In the Japanese Martial Arts the training sessions commence with bowing, and the etiquette tends to be very formal and strict. The instructor is always addressed as 'Sensei' (Japanese for master) rather than by his personal name. Surprisingly this formality and discipline seems to appeal to all students without exception.

The act of bowing is a sign of acceptance, reverence, acknowledgment, and submission. In the Martial Arts it represents an acknowledgment of the sensei as an instructor and master. A second bow quite often means an acceptance of the shrine and all that that represents. On the main wall may be hung the Associations symbol, or in Japan there would be situated a small Buddhist or Shinto shrine. The shrine may house a flower, or a fine sword, a scroll or flag. Whatever is on the shrine will be a treasured item. The bow is a sign of respect, the equivalent of crossing oneself on entering a Catholic Church. Remember that Nippon is over all the Japanese Martial Arts.

When the lesson is about to begin, the students will line up facing the sensei, whereupon they will bow again. This bow has to be performed in a particular way; the head, body, arms, and legs have to be in the correct position from all angles. The 'dojo' is considered to be a sacred place so all behaviour should be governed by this fact. Profanity, loud talking, socialising and any misbehaviour are out of place. All the time must be used wisely and concentrated on development of the mind and body either by training or by meditation.

Training in some of the styles of the arts will then call for the students to sit 'Za Zen' (sitting meditation) with eyes closed, and concentration on the correct posture and breath control. This will continue for some time. A similar procedure may take place at the end of a session as well. Maybe an oath or motto will be spoken, such as:

1. We will train our hearts and bodies for a firm un-shaken spirit.
2. We will pursue the true meaning of the martial way so that in time our senses may be alert.
3. With true vigour we will seek to cultivate a spirit of self-denial.
4. We will observe the rules of courtesy, respect our superiors, and refrain from violence.
5. We will follow our gods and Buddha, and never forget the virtue of humility.
6. We will look upwards to wisdom and strength, not seeking other's desires.
7. All our lives through the discipline of Karate we will seek to fulfil the true meaning of 'the way'.

Sentiments such as these coming from a Karate Club appear to a Westerner as misplaced, or even possibly hypocritical, but in fact in the majority of cases the students are perfectly serious, and do in fact spend their lives trying to live up to these ideals. Unfortunately, there are some whose very nature preclude them from always keeping the promise to refrain from violence. The very training aiming at automatic reaction is such, that in some circumstances the violent action comes first and the thought after.

Chapter 11

Ki or Chi Power

Group training is often accompanied by a shouting chant initiated by the sensei. His shout alternates with the shouting response of the students. This shouting will continue with a rising energy and power. The word that is shouted is 'kiai', and each shout will be accompanied by a particular physical stance. The continuing chanting produces a semi-hypnotic effect on the students, and the sensei can utilise this effect to lead and control the class. To chant well and keep in time is very important and requires imagination and sensitivity. The overall effect is to strengthen and develop ki power. Ki is Japanese, chi is Chinese. This power can be developed to an incredible degree and is a basic neccessity in most of the Martial Arts.

In the soft styles the power is certainly present but does not manifest itself in physical power. It is a development of an inner power and concentration which is just as powerful but without the visible manifestation. The ability to summon up this power uses the body's vital energy flow, and is an integral part of the training. Breathing techniques also contribute to heighten this power especially in certain movements, and in the determination to win a competition bout.

It is this same power that is utilised in acupuncture and acupressure, and various other alternative healing methods. The root power is just the same. It is believed that acupuncture in particular links in to the 'Life Force' which is believed to be in every human being. This force follows certain channels and roots in the body and forms the basis of study in Chinese medicine. It must be stated that this power (as with most powers) can be used for both good and evil. Yin and Yang represent what is good and what is evil; both light and dark. The dark side of ki power is an energy that can kill; the light side is believed to heal.

The more advanced a practitioner becomes in the Martial Arts and the longer the time spent in concentrating both in meditation and practice of the breathing techniques, the stronger becomes the ki power. This internal energy invades the mind, actions, and automatic system until such a time as the correct movement can follow the attacking stance or movement of an opponent with the stirring up of inner power ready to protect from an assailant. This action can take place without any conscious prior thought having taken place. Ki is a super-power wilfully stirred up and practised; to be tapped into and used when so desired. Abnormal amounts of energy and strength are utilised with ki power as have been demonstrated by practitioners breaking pieces of wood etc. with their bare hands.

One story tells of top instructor Koichi Tohei demonstrating this power by allowing arrows to be fired at him from a distance of less than 6 metres. He calmly stood and fended off the arrows with his hands without one arrow touching him.

Another incident took place on British television on a programme called *You Bet* on 27th September, 1991. A Martial Art student accepted a challenge to break approximately 100 roof tiles in one and a half minutes. The tiles were placed in groups, each group being made up of two supports about three to four inches (10 cm) high, and about one foot (23 cm) apart. On top of each pile lay a piece of felt to protect the competitor's hands from damage. On estimate one could assume that there were five tiles on each of twenty piles which were lined up in a square.

Down each side of the square stood three helpers dressed in Martial Arts uniform. These attendants were ready to bring to the front of the square any unbroken tiles. These were set up in piles for the competitor to break at the end of the sequence.

Before the challenge commenced a chorus of shouts of 'kiai' went up from the assistants, answered by a similar shout from the competitor. This shouting continued with each shout becoming greater in volume and strength. Suddenly the shouting stopped. The ki power had been built up and the competition started. The sequence of action was fast and violent. All of the tiles were broken within the required time of one and a half minutes.

It so happened that an interested engineer decided to replay the action of this event very slowly so to observe the competitor's action in breaking the tiles. To the engineer's total amazement, he discovered that in fact the tiles were never touched; the force of ki power broke the tiles without ever coming in contact with the competitor's hand. That was the force and power of ki.

Ki power is not a force to be taken lightly and there is a danger of this power being misused. The strength of ki power is totally demonic and allows the advanced student to take blows and kicks that would normally be beyond human beings to take without serious damage to their bodies. Besides the possibility of physical damage to participants, sometimes of a very serious nature, there is the long-term effect for those who become Christians, with the subsequent battle between the light of Christ and the darkness of the demonic, and satanic infiltration from the practice of the Martial Arts. The power of ki can surface very suddenly and violently in every-day life, if a student of the Martial Arts comes under an unexpected attack. This unprovoked verbal attack can stir up the ki power in such a way that it could explode violently in power and physical strength, and the outcome could be a serious one. Until such time arrives when the Martial Arts can be dealt with by teaching and deliverance, the exponent is in danger of reacting violently on occasion.

In releasing captives from the demonic power in the Martial Arts, God's power which is greater than all other powers, is able to free and completely release all those who turn to God and His Son Jesus Christ in complete acceptance of the truth as John 8:31&32 says:

> *'Jesus said "If you abide in My word, you are my disciples indeeed. And you shall know the truth, and the truth shall make you free."'*

The following two passages speak clearly of the power of God which is above and beyond all other power. The raising of Jesus Christ from the dead stands as a reminder to Satan that he is a lesser power no matter how he chooses to lead people into thinking he is the greatest, and his end is clearly written in the book of Revelation. He cannot deny that, try as he might.

> *'Therefore I also, after I heard of your faith in the Lord Jesus and your love for all the saints, do not cease to give thanks for you, making mention in my prayers; that the God of our Lord Jesus Christ the Father of glory, may give to you the spirit of wisdom and revelation in the knowledge of Him. The eyes of your understanding being enlightened; that you may know what is the hope of His calling, what are the riches of the glory of His inheritance in the saints, and what is the exceeding greatness of His power towards us who believe, according to the working of His mighty power which He worked in Christ when He raised Him from the dead and seated Him at His right hand in the heavenly places, far above all pricipality and power and might and dominion, and every name that is named, not only in this age but also that which is to come. And He put*

all things under His feet, and gave Him to be head over all things to the Church which is His body, the fullness of Him who fills all in all.' (Ephesians 1:15–23)

'To whom then will you liken me, or to whom shall I be equal? says the Holy One. Lift up your eyes on high, and see who has created these things, who brings out their host by number; He calls them all by name, by the greatness of His might and the strength of His power not one is missing.' (Isaiah 40:25&26)

Chapter 12

Finding Freedom

A number of people have enquired how to set about releasing someone from the demonic hold of Yoga and the Martial Arts, therefore this chapter contains specific suggestions as a guide for experienced counsellors. Please do not counsel anyone on your own, but always with a co-counsellor and if possible with a counsellor of the opposite sex. If a stripping away of the lesser points for release are dealt with first, this should minimize the reaction from the counsellee and effect a smoother release.

One very important aspect of helping someone to find freedom from the practice of ungodly beliefs or pursuits, is the control over the mind from the practise of the particular medium that has been pursued. With the infiltration of ungodly practises, whether by physical action or verbal utterance, there will be a need to release the mind from all that has entered from the basic source of belief and acceptance of anything concerning that belief.

As with all counselling situations one commences by going over the counsellee's past and dealing with all instances of sin in that person's life, encouraging the faint hearted and speaking God's forgiveness on all confessed sin. One area of great importance is making quite sure that the counsellee understands how to maintain the armour of God written of in Ephesians 6. If this subject is not understood, the counsellee will have great difficulty maintaining any freedom from the counselling. It is necessary to explain to those Christians who do not know of this teaching the reason for this subject. A good way of explaining this teaching is to use the following illustration.

Those of us living in areas of high security risk do not leave our house or flat without locking the door. Neither do we leave a window open as an invitation for those looking for an easy entry. Neither do we go around with money in our hands ready to be snatched. We protect our property and our possessions from an invader of any type. So Christians should always wear the armour of God as written of in Ephesians. These words are written becuase it is a fact that the enemy is prowling around looking for a weakness – an opportunity for entrance. The armour represents various things and is written of in poetic language to make it easier to effect. If it was unnecessary for us to have this protection from demonic infiltration, why are there so many references and descriptions in the Bible concerning protective armour? (Isaiah 59; Romans 13:12; Ephesians 6; 1 Thessalonians 5:8, and many other sources.)

For experienced counsellors I am providing a list of suggestions of the particular areas which need to be addressed in counselling someone who has been involved in the Martial Arts or Yoga. The depth of ministry will be in accordance with the level of training in each case.

Each counselling session should commence with a confession of faith in God Almighty and His Son Jesus Christ. This is not to doubt the counsellee's faith in God but for the enemy to hear. The stronger the counsellee's faith in God the easier will be the release.

1. The counsellee needs to have a real desire to be set free.
2. There has to be a complete confession of all sin.
3. Forgiveness of anyone the counsellee may hold anything against.

4. A genuine statement and declaration of faith.
5. An invitation for the Holy Spirit to be present.
6. Release from Mars the Roman god of war, who is over all the Martial Arts.
7. A renouncing and releasing from the particular name of the Martial Art and type of Yoga practised.
8. A cutting off and releasing from every move, and from every position practised in either the Martial Arts or Yoga.
9. A cutting off and releasing from any mantra or object used to aid meditation.
10. A cutting off from all instructors by name.
11. A cutting off from the name of the practice hall.
12. A releasing and cutting off from all signs of respect by bowing prior to a Martial Art bout or following a bout.
13. A cutting off and freeing from any symbol seen or unseen in the meeting hall; i.e. a flag, scroll, picture etc.
14. Confession of being a part of a practice of a physical nature eminating from an Eastern religion, and a releasing from the same.
15. A releasing from the Yin and Yang symbols and all that they represent.
16. Confession of injuries caused to others during any practice of any Martial Art, and a prayer for healing of the injured party.
17. A cutting off and confession of any commitments made verbally or, in writing concerning the Martial Arts or Yoga.
18. A cutting off from all breathing exercises and any subsequent ill-effect on the lungs etc.
19. A cutting off from all ki or chi power.
20. A cutting off from names of all animals represented in either the Martial Arts or Yoga.
21. Break the power of every belt award, and speak God's freedom to the pariciant and freedom from slavery from any aspect of the Martial Arts.

22. Invite God's healing and release to the person's mind and spirit, and pray for a conversion of the mind and spirit to the mind of God.

This is a suggested list and not comprehensive. One other item for those who have practised Ju-jitsu; a move of twisting the uniform jacket at the neck, and pressing the thumb against the throat is called 'a Juju jimmie' and needs the spirit of throttling delivered. This move is sometimes used in other mediums. All injuries to the counsellee will need dealing with as well.

Remember:

> *'The word of God is living and powerful, and sharper than any two-edged sword, piercing even to the division of soul and spirit, and of joints and marrow, and is a discerner of the thoughts and intents of the heart. And there is no creature hidden from His sight, but all things are naked and open to the eyes of Him to whom we must give an account.'* (Hebrews 4:12&13)

Extra to the list for deliverance are one or two other areas to address, but as these affect demonic entry of other types of involvement I am listing them separately. With any acknowledgment of other faith systems and practice of meditation, prayers and other actions particular to that medium or faith, there will be a physical control needing release – the automatic nervous system; the central nervous system; the glands, especially the adrenal; every muscle; the conscious, semi-conscious and unconscious mind; the will and that part of the mind particularly that makes decisions. With the breathing apparatus it is helpful to invite the counsellee to breathe in the breath of God deep into their lungs and then command any unclean thing to come out with their breath.

I would like to conclude with a word of encouragement to those prepared to be involved in releasing other Brothers and Sisters from the enemy's hold. This is a precious ministry and not to be taken lightly, but if there is a strong desire for the captive to be set free, then may the dear Lord bless you in your work for Him. Do not be afraid, but in faith stand against the work of the demonic. The devil is far more frightened by the power of God in you than you need to be of him. This is the Lord's work; we are His ministers and He will not let us down. The devil and his hordes can be very legalistic insisting you come against the correct area, but keep in there and do ask the counsellee to let you know what is going on in his mind. This is the way the enemy works.

> *'These things I have spoken to you while being present with you. But the helper, the Holy Spirit whom the Father will send in my name, he will teach you all things, and bring to your remembrance all things that I said to you. Peace I leave with you, my peace I give to you; not as the world gives do I give to you. Let not your heart be troubled neither let it be afraid.'*

(John 14:25–27)

Glossary

Acupuncture – Chinese system of healing using needles at key points of the body.

Atemi – Japanese for the vital points of the body, which when attacked can cause pain, injury or even death.

Black belt – The level of proficiency in Martial Arts at which a student may graduate to instructor.

Bokken or Bokuto – A wooden sword used for training in Japanese Martial Arts.

Cat stance – Used in Kung Fu and Karate. The weight is placed on the back leg.

Centreline – The imaginary line of Wing Chun Kung Fu which runs down the centre of the body, the focus of attack and defence.

Ch'an – Chinese for Zen, or meditation.

Chi – Internal force or energy which is harnessed, in particular by practitioners of Tai Chi Chuan and Hsing-i.

Chudan – The chest area of Japanese Martial Arts.

Dan – Japanese for degree, denoting rank of black belt.

Dim mak – Death touch, or strike to a vital point causing delayed injury or death.

Do – Japanese for path or way, also used as a suffix, e.g. Kendo.

Dobok – Korean for practice suit.

Do jang – Korean for training hall.

Dojo – Japanese for training hall.

Escrima – Spanish for 'skirmish'. Filipino system employing sticks, swords and daggers.

Five animals – Movements of the crane, dragon, leopard, tiger and snake incorporated into the Shaolin fighting systems.

Gi – Training uniform for Japanese Martial Arts. In Korean it means 'spirit'.

Gup – In Taekwon-do one of the ten grades below black belt.

Hakama – Long divided skirt used in some Japanese Martial Arts, notably Aikido and Kendo.

Hara-kiri – Japanese ritual suicide by disembowelment, the ultimate act of atonement.

Horse stance – Strong basic stance of both Chinese and Japanese styles.

I ching – Ancient Chinese book of divination, whose philosophical principles form the basis of Tai chi, Pa-kua and Hsing-i.

Ippon – Used in Japanese contests to denote a full point.

Judoka – One who practises Judo.

Jutsu or Jitsu – Japanese for skill or art, also used as a suffix e.g. Kenjutsu.

Karate-ka – One who practises Karate.

Kata – A pattern or form of moves in which the Japanese martial artist fights imaginary opponents.

Katana – A Japanese sword.

Ki – Japanese for chi, internal energy vital to the practice of Aikido and Hapkido.

Kiai – Powerful shout of Japanese Martial Arts which can stun an opponent or give extra impetus to a technique.

Kote – Kendo gauntlet.

Kup so – Vital spot in Taekwon-do.

Kwoon – Chinese for training hall.

Kyu – Japanese for any grade below shodan (1st degree black belt).

Martial Arts – The arts of war, from Mars god of war.

Men – Kendo helmet.

Oos – A form of greeting used in the dojo.

Randori – Free sparring of Judo.

Ryu – Japanese for school or style.

Samurai – 'One who serves' – the knightly warrior of feudal Japan.

Sensei – Japanese for master.

Shiatsu – Japanese finger pressure therapy.

Shinai – Bamboo sword made of four strips bound together. Replaces the live blade in Kendo.

Sumotori – Sumo wrestlers.

Tanden – Japanese for navel, thought to be the source of power.

Tare – Apron, part of Kendo armour, to protect the vital points below the waist.

Te – Okinawan for hand, as in Karate, empty hand.

Tenugui – Headband used in Kendo to absorb perspiration.

White belt – This denotes beginner in several Japanese systems.

Waza-ari – A half point in Japanese competition.

Yang – The positive male principle of Chinese.

Yin – The passive female principle of Chinese.

Yoi – Ready position in Japanese Martial Arts.

Zanshin – A state of calm alertness cultivated in Japanese Martial Arts.

Zen – Religious philosophy that claims one can reach satori (enlightenment through meditation).

Additional Information on Martial Arts

Kung Fu Styles

Tai Chi Chuan
Pa-kua
Hsing-I
The Praying Mantis – This style is from Sil Lum – a Shaolin style of Kung Fu which involves, grabbing, pulling, striking, and short quick foot movements with kicking to the groin area and kneecap.
Wing Chun (also called Street Fighting) – This style uses a weapon called a Luk-dim-boun-kwan – a pole approximately 3 metres long.

Karate Styles

Shotokan
Kyokushinkai
Wado-ryu
Shito-ryu
Shukokai
Sankukai
Shotokai
Goyuryu
Goju-kai
Uechi-ryu

Japanese Martial Arts Using Weapons

Kendo – Shinai, a bamboo sword made of four strips bound together, used in place of a live blade.

Iai-do – Based on swordsmanship.

Kyudo – 'The way of the bow'. The bow is about 2 metres long.

Yabusame – Horseback archery.

Unarmed Styles

Aikido
 – *Yoshinkan Aikido*: A lesser known style.
 – *Tomiki Aikido*
 – *Ju Jitsu*
 – *Kuatsu*
 – *Judo*
 – *Shorinji Kempo*: A mixture of Karate and Aikido.

Sumo Wrestling

The Korean Martial Arts

Taekwon-do
Hapkido
Tang Soo Do

Martial Arts from Various Countries

Thai Boxing – A very lethal form of boxing with kicks from elbow, foot, or knee and aimed at the stomach area. Flying kicks are also used.

Burma Bando – Based on the moves of twelve animals, this form may sometimes use weapons.

Malaysian Bersilat – A method of self-defence mostly called by a shortened version to 'silat'.

Brazilian Capoira – The roots of this style come out of slavery and are mainly defence moves. This is an acrobatic style, but has become a killing style with 72 moves.

Filipino Kali (meaning blade or knife) – The knife is called a 'bolo' and is similar to a machete.

Escrima – This form developed from Kali and is now practised in Europe.

Russian Sambo Wrestling – The main objective of this form is to seize the legs of the opponent and throw them to the ground. This is claimed to have originated in China.

Indian Kalaripayit – A training method for battle.

French, La Savate – A kicking style, which includes hitting with an open palm.

Pizza (tut - 450757.

Bibliography

Barclay, William. *The Plain Man Looks at the Beatitudes*. Collins Fount Publications.

Cuyler, P.L. *From Rite to Sport*. Weatherhill Publications.

Donovan, Ticky. *Traditional Karate*. Pelham Press.

Enroth, Ronald. *Evangelising the Cults*. Word Publishing.

Eyre, Ronald. *The Long Search*. British Broadcasting Company.

Ferrie, Eddie. *Judo for Self-Defence*. The Cromwood Press.

Goldman, John. *Taekwondo. Guiness Publishing*.

Iyengar, B.K.S. *The Concise Light on Yoga*. Unwin Paperbacks.

Kellar, Phillip. *A Shepherd Looks at the 23rd Psalm*. Marshall Pickering: HarperCollins Publishers.

Lewis, Jesse Penn. *War on the Saints*. Diasozo Trust; Thomas E. Lowe Ltd. Publishers, New York.

Lewis, Peter. *The Way to the Martial Arts*. Marshall Cavendish Books Ltd.

Mercier, S.C. *Hinduism*. Themes in Religion: Longman.

McDowell J. and Stewart, Don. *Concise Guide to Today's Religions*. Scripture Press.

Palmer, Martin. *Taoism*. Published by Element.

Quinn, Kaleghl. *Stand Your Ground*. Channel Four Book: Orbis Publishing Ltd.

Schmidt, Richard J. and Hesson James L. *Karate*. Sport for Life: Scott Foreman and Co.

Williams, Bryn. *Know TaekWondo* and *Know Karate-do*. William Luscombe Publisher Ltd.

Worthington, Vivian. *A History of Yoga*. Arkana: Published by Penguin Group.